200 mini cakes and bakes

hamlyn | all colour cookbook

200 mini cakes and bakes

An Hachette UK Company
www.hachette.co.uk

First published in Great Britain in 2010 by Hamlyn
a division of Octopus Publishing Group Ltd, Endeavour
House, 189 Shaftesbury Avenue, London, WC2H 8JY
www.octopusbooks.co.uk

ISBN 13: 978-0-600-62269-7

A CIP catalogue record for this book is available
from the British Library.

Printed and bound in China

10 9 8 7 6 5 4 3 2

Both metric and imperial measurements have been given
in all recipes. Use one set of measurements only, and not a
mixture of both.

Standard level spoon measurements are used in all recipes.
1 tablespoon = one 15 ml spoon
1 teaspoon = one 5 ml spoon

Ovens should be preheated to the specified temperature
– if using a fan-assisted oven, follow the manufacturer's
instructions for adjusting the time and temperature.

Fresh herbs should be used unless otherwise stated.

Medium eggs should be used unless otherwise stated.

The Department of Health advises that eggs should not
be consumed raw. This book contains some dishes made
with raw or lightly cooked eggs. It is prudent for vulnerable
people such as pregnant and nusing mothers, invalids,
the elderly, babies and young children to avoid uncooked
or lightly cooked dishes made with eggs. Once prepared,
these dishes should be kept refrigerated and used promptly.

This book includes dishes made with nuts and nut
derivatives. It is advisable for those with known allergic
reactions to nuts and nut derivatives and those who may
be potentially vulnerable to these allergies to avoid dishes
made with nuts and nut oils. It is also prudent to check the
labels of pre-prepared ingredients for the possible
inclusion of nut derivatives.

contents

introduction   6

cupcakes   16

biscuits & cookies   66

slices & traybakes   98

pastries   126

meringues & macaroons   160

scones & other mini cakes   184

treats for kids   208

index   236

acknowledgements   240

introduction

introduction

Baking continues to maintain its appeal as a thoroughly rewarding form of cooking, and there are plenty of reasons why baking 'mini' cakes has a particular appeal. We don't always want a great hunk of chocolate sponge or fruit pie but a small 'taster' portion of a sweet morsel that's packed with flavour and is reassuringly and comfortingly sweet. Some of the cakes such as the muffins and simple cupcakes are quick to make, ideal for a family treat at any time of day, while others are more time consuming and best made for a special occasion. Because of their size, some of the bakes are intentionally richer and more flavour intensive than larger cakes, perfect for passing round after a special supper or at the end of a drinks and nibbles party. A selection of several mini cakes in contrasting flavours and textures makes a stunning display that'll attract plenty of appreciative tasters for this sort of entertaining. Manageable little morsels that are so easy to just pop in the mouth!

equipment

A glance around any large cook shop will reveal a huge variety of equipment specially designed for baking mini cakes in all shapes and sizes. Very little of this equipment is essential for most of the recipes in this book, although you might be interested in collecting a small stash of utensils, tins and other gadgets that will make baking easier and help achieve professional-looking results.

mini cupcake & muffin tins

These vary in tray size and capacity and are available in metal or silicone. They're ideal for making small tartlets or for lining with mini paper muffin or cupcake cases.

madeleine tins

Shell shaped to create delicate Madeleine sponges, these sectioned tins are available in metal or silicone. The madeleine sponge mixture can also be cooked in mini bun tins.

mini loaf tins

Ideal for small sponge- or bread-based recipes, these little loaves always look impressive. If you only have a few of the tins you'll need to bake the cakes in batches, or use a sectioned silicone loaf tray.

loose-based baking tins

Some of the recipes are baked in small square, loose-based tins. Regular, deep loose-based cake tins can be used although shallow square tart tins, usually about 3 cm (1¼ inches) deep are easier to manage.

dariole, brioche and tartlet tins

With a base diameter of about 3 cm (1¼ inches) these are perfect for mini cakes. They're usually sold individually and can be expensive if buying plenty, but you can always bake in batches as they're so quick to cook. If buying tartlet tins, loose-based ones are easier to use as you can push the tartlet cases out of the tins from underneath without damaging the delicate pastry.

paper cake cases

There are so many different sizes of cake cases in a feast of striking colours. For mini cakes choose ones with a base measurement of 3–4cm (1¼–1¾ inches), which is considerably smaller than a regular cupcake case. You'll need to use a bun or mini muffin tray with similar-sized sections as the paper alone isn't enough to support the filling.

mini silicone muffin cases

Brightly coloured or pastel-shaded silicone mini muffin or cupcake cases are increasingly popular. You have a reusable supply at hand and you don't need a sectioned tin for cooking as they sit on a regular baking sheet. (See using silicone mini muffin cases below.)

piping bags

Reusable nylon piping bags, available from specialist cake-decorating shops or cook shops, can be fitted with a star or plain metal or plastic piping nozzle for piping, then washed and thoroughly dried before storing. They're ideal for piping large swirls of cream or frosting for decorating, or for piping meringues neatly before baking. Large disposable polythene bags are also useful for piping large amounts and the ends of the bags are snipped off to accommodate the nozzles. For piping decorations such as melted chocolate a paper piping bag is ideal.

piping nozzles

The recipes in this book use plain and star nozzles with a tip measurement of

about 1 cm (½ inch) in diameter for piping meringues, biscuit dough, creams and frostings. They're available in metal and plastic; metal ones give a better finish.

hand-held electric whisks
These are perfect for mixing smaller quantities of sponge, cream and icings and are a useful tool. Mixing can also be done by handusing a balloon whisk although it'll require a little more effort to achieve the right consistency.

biscuit cutters
Several recipes require small cutters, usually round or heart shaped and between about 3 and 6 cm (1¼ and 2½ inches) in diameter. There are many other cutter shapes available and you can easily adapt biscuit designs to make them seasonal, for example spring flowers, Christmas stocking, etc.

using silicone muffin cases
Arrange silicone cases on a baking sheet, spacing them slightly apart and fill as you would a paper case. After baking leave the cakes to cool in the cases, or, if you want to remove them for serving, allow to cool for 2–5 minutes and then lift the cakes out onto a wire rack to cool. The cases are dishwasher-proof but are likely to fly around during the cycle as they're so light. You'll probably find it easier to wash them by hand. After washing it's easiest to let them drain and dry thoroughly, upturned, on a tea towel so they're thoroughly dry before stacking and storing.

making & using a paper piping bag
Cut out a 25 cm (10 inch) square of greaseproof paper. Fold it diagonally in half. Cut the paper in half, just to one side of the

folded line. Holding one piece with the long edge away from you, curl the right-hand point over to meet the centre point, making a cone shape. Bring the left-hand point over the cone so the three points meet. Fold the points over several times to secure the cone. Snip off the tip and insert a piping nozzle, if using. Half fill the bag and fold over the ends to secure. If using the bag without a piping nozzle, fill the bag and fold over the open end to secure as above and then snip off the merest tip with scissors. Test how thickly the filling flows from the bag and snip off a little more from the bag if you want to pipe thicker lines.

cake-making methods

There are different processes used to make various types of cakes from sponges to meringues. These guidelines will help:

mixing sponges

Most of the sponge cakes in the book are made using the 'all in one' method in which all the ingredients are simple whisked together before adding any additional ingredients like nuts, chocolate or dried fruit. Soften the butter in the mixing bowl first (see page 14) and then simply beat all the ingredients together. This usually takes between 1 and 2 minutes and the consistency of the beaten ingredients will become paler in colour and develop a soft, creamy consistency.

making muffins

Muffins are made by folding the wet ingredients such as eggs, milk, yogurt and melted butter into the dry ones, which you've already combined in a bowl. Once the wet

ingredients are added, use a large metal spoon and gently stir the ingredients together. Mix until they're only just combined so traces of flour are still visible. Overbeating will produce tough results.

making meringues

Use thoroughly clean, dry equipment for making meringues as any grease will prevent the egg whites from peaking. Whisk the egg whites until stiff so that they form firm peaks when the whisk is lifted from the bowl. Add a tablespoonful of the sugar and whisk for about 10 seconds before adding another tablespoonful of sugar. Repeat until all the sugar has been incorporated. The meringue should be stiff and glossy. If the sugar is added too quickly the sugar syrup will seep out during baking.

shaping scones

The easiest mistake to make when shaping scones is to roll the dough too thinly so they're flat and biscuity. The dough once mixed should be soft but not sticky and unmanageable. Tip it onto a lightly floured surface and roll out thickly. Where as regular scone dough is rolled to about 2.5 cm (1 inch) thickness, mini scones are rolled slightly thinner to about 1.5 cm (¾ inch) therefore, as smaller shapes are cut and the baking time will be shorter.

using filo pastry

Filo pastry dries out very quickly so always keep any sheets you are not using wrapped in clingfilm or coverered with a damp cloth to stop it turning brittle and flaky. You don't need to grease tins before lining with filo pastry but you do need to brush each layer with butter or oil so the baked pastries are moist and sufficiently flavoured.

baking & decorating techniques

Here are a few simple guidelines for queries that you might have related to baking and decorating, particularly if you're a first-timer.

softening butter

Unless the weather is very hot or the kitchen is really warm, butter is still slightly too firm to use even if it's been out of the fridge a while. For sponge-based cakes and buttercream, cut the measured butter into small pieces and soften in the microwave.

Use medium power and heat in short bursts until the butter is soft enough to be pushed into with your finger. Take care not to leave it too long or it'll melt completely.

melting chocolate

There are three ways of melting chocolate to use for decorating cakes or adding to other ingredients for icings and cake mixes.
To melt on the hob, chop the chocolate into small pieces and put in a heatproof bowl. Rest the bowl over a pan of very gently simmering water, making sure the base of the bowl doesn't come in contact with the water. Once the chocolate starts to melt, turn off the heat and leave until completely melted, stirring once or twice until no lumps remain. Don't let any water get into the bowl, for example steam from the pan, or the chocolate will solidify and cannot be melted again.
To melt in the microwave, chop the chocolate

into small pieces and put in a heatproof bowl. Melt the chocolate in one-minute spurts, checking frequently. Take care, particularly when melting white or milk chocolate as they have a higher fat and sugar content and are more likely to scorch.
To melt in the oven, chop the chocolate into small pieces and put in a small ovenproof dish or bowl. Put in the switched off oven after baking and leave until melted.

Sometimes chocolate is melted with other ingredients such as butter, syrup or milk. Check more frequently as the melting time will usually be quicker.

lining tins

Sponge-based cakes and traybakes usually require greaseproof or nonstick baking paper lined tins. Brush the tin with melted butter first, then cut a length of paper that is long enough to cover the base of the tin and come up two sides. Press into position. Cut two further rectangles to line the ends of the tin. Grease the paper so the cake mixture is not prevented from rising by sticking to the paper.

filling paper or silicone cases

Cake mixtures rise as they bake so don't over-fill the cases or the mixture will spill over the sides during baking. Unless a recipe states otherwise fill the cases with sponge mixture so they're no more than two-thirds full. If you have excess mixture, bake a second batch to save wastage. If baking muffins you can pile the mixture up a little more in the centre.

baking blind

Pastry tartlet cases are usually baked 'blind' before filling so the pastry is partially cooked and crisped up before the filling is added. Once you've lined the cases with pastry, cut circles of greaseproof or nonstick baking paper about 5 cm (2 inches) larger than the cases and push down into the cases. Fill with baking beans (available from cook shops) or with a dry ingredient such as lentils or beans that you can label and reuse for this purpose. After the pastry is baked, lift out the paper and beans. The pastry is then usually baked for a further few minutes before filling.

whipping cream

It's very easy to over whip double cream for use as a filling or decoration whether used alone or flavoured with other ingredients. It's flavour becomes less creamy and the texture grainy. Use a hand-held electric whisk or balloon whisk and beat the cream until it only just starts to hold its shape. Bear in mind that the cream will continue to thicken up even as you spread it or transfer it to a piping bag.

storing cakes and mini bakes

Most mini cakes, biscuits and pastries are best served freshly baked. However, if you want to make them ahead, they can be stored in an airtight container for up to 24 hours before serving. Sponge-based cakes can be frozen and thawed completely before decorating. Muffins and scones are always best served freshly baked, even still slightly

warm from the oven. Alternatively, make them ahead and freeze for reheating in the oven to revive their freshly baked texture and flavour. Crisp meringues and macaroons have a longer storage life. Undecorated they will store for several days before sandwiching with fillings or whipped cream.

royal icing

Made with royal icing sugar, which is superfine, and does not clog, so is suitable for more elaborate decoration work. For 1 quantity to use in the recipes, beat 200g (7oz) royal icing sugar in a bowl with 1 egg white to make icing with a softly peaking consistency.

cupcakes

lemon & limoncello cupcakes

Makes **16**
Preparation time **20 minutes**,
plus cooling
Cooking time **12 minutes**

65 g (2½ oz) **lightly salted butter**, softened
65 g (2½ oz) **caster sugar**
65 g (2½ oz) **self-raising flour**
finely grated rind of 1 **lemon**, plus 1 tablespoon of the juice
1 **egg**
3 tablespoons **limoncello liqueur**

Icing
5 tablespoons **lemon curd**
75 g (3 oz) **unsalted butter**, softened
50 g (2 oz) **icing sugar**, plus extra for dusting

Place 16 mini silicone muffin cases on a baking sheet.

Put the butter, sugar, flour, lemon rind and egg in a bowl and beat with a hand-held electric whisk until light and creamy. Divide among the cases.

Bake in a preheated oven, 180°C (350°F), Gas Mark 4, for 10–12 minutes until risen and just firm. Leave in the cases for 2 minutes, then transfer to a wire rack to cool. Drizzle 2 tablespoons of the limoncello over the cakes and leave to cool completely.

Reserve 2 tablespoons of the lemon curd and spread the remainder over the cakes with a palette knife.

Make the icing by putting the unsalted butter, icing sugar, reserved limoncello, reserved lemon curd and the lemon juice in a bowl and beating well until smooth and creamy. Place in a piping bag fitted with a star nozzle and pipe swirls on top of each cake. Serve lightly dusted with icing sugar.

For rhubarb & orange cupcakes, make the sponge as above, using the finely grated rind of ½ orange instead of lemon. Divide among the cases. Cut 100 g (3½ oz) rhubarb into very thin diagonal slices and toss with 4 teaspoons caster sugar and a good pinch of ground ginger. Pile on top of the sponge bases and scatter with 2 tablespoons crushed flaked almonds. Bake as above and serve dusted with icing sugar.

very chocolatey muffins

Makes **16**
Preparation time **10 minutes**
Cooking time **15 minutes**

100 g (3½ oz) **self-raising flour**
25 g (1 oz) **cocoa powder**
½ teaspoon **baking powder**
50 g (2 oz) **light muscovado sugar**
100 g (3½ oz) **milk chocolate**, chopped
1 **egg**
5 tablespoons **milk**
50 g (2 oz) **lightly salted butter**, melted

Place 16 mini silicone muffin cases on a baking sheet.

Sift the flour, cocoa powder and baking powder into a bowl. Stir in the sugar and chopped chocolate.

Beat the egg in a separate bowl and stir in the milk and melted butter. Add to the dry ingredients using a large metal spoon, stir the ingredients together until only just combined. Divide among the cases.

Bake in a preheated oven, 200°C (400°F), Gas Mark 6, for 15 minutes until risen and just firm. Serve warm or cold.

For spiced pear muffins, sift 100 g (3½ oz) self-raising flour and ½ teaspoon ground mixed spice into a bowl and stir in 25 g (1 oz) oatmeal, ½ teaspoon baking powder and 50 g (2 oz) golden caster sugar. Peel, core and dice 1 ripe pear and add to the bowl with 25 g (1 oz) sultanas. Mix together the egg, milk and butter as above and add to the bowl. Divide among the cases and bake as above. Serve dusted with icing sugar.

blueberry friands

Makes **16**
Preparation time **10 minutes**
Cooking time **15 minutes**

50 g (2 oz) **lightly salted butter**
2 **egg whites**
25 g (1 oz) **plain flour**
75 g (3 oz) **icing sugar**, plus extra for dusting
40 g (1½ oz) **ground almonds**
½ teaspoon **almond extract**
50 g (2 oz) **blueberries**

Place 16 mini silicone muffin cases on a baking sheet.

Melt the butter and leave to cool. Whisk the egg whites in a thoroughly clean bowl until frothy but not turning white and peaking.

Sift the flour and icing sugar into the bowl, then add the ground almonds. Stir the almond extract into the melted butter and add to the bowl. Using a large metal spoon, stir the ingredients gently together until combined. Divide among the cases so each is about three-quarters full and place several blueberries on top of each.

Bake in a preheated oven, 200°C (400°F), Gas Mark 6, for 12–15 minutes until risen and just firm to the touch. Leave in the cases for 5 minutes, then transfer to a wire rack to cool. Serve warm or cold dusted with icing sugar.

For hazelnut & apricot friands, lightly toast 40 g (1½ oz) hazelnuts and grind in a food processor. Chop 50 g (2 oz) plump dried apricots into very small pieces. Prepare the cakes as above using the hazelnuts instead of the almonds, vanilla extract instead of the almond extract and placing a little pile of chopped apricots on the centres instead of the blueberries.

marsala raisin coffee muffins

Makes **16**
Preparation time **15 minutes**,
plus soaking
Cooking time **12 minutes**

50 g (2 oz) **raisins**
4 tablespoons **marsala**
1 teaspoon instant **espresso coffee powder**
2 teaspoons **boiling water**
125 g (4 oz) **self-raising flour**
½ teaspoon **baking powder**
65 g (2½ oz) **golden caster sugar**
125 g (4 oz) **natural yogurt**
1 **egg**, beaten
2 tablespoons **vegetable oil**

Icing
½ teaspoon **espresso coffee powder**
1½ teaspoons **hot water**
40 g (1½ oz) **icing sugar**, sifted

Put the raisins and marsala in a small saucepan and heat until hot but not boiling. Pour into a bowl and leave to stand for 2 hours until the raisins have plumped up.

Place 16 mini silicone muffin cases on a baking sheet.

Mix the coffee powder with the measurement water. Sift the flour and baking powder into a bowl. Stir in the sugar.

Mix together the yogurt, egg, oil and coffee mixture and stir in the raisins and any unabsorbed liquid. Add to the dry ingredients. Using a large metal spoon, stir the ingredients together until only just combined. Divide among the cases.

Bake in a preheated oven, 200°C (400°F), Gas Mark 6, for about 12 minutes until risen and firm. Leave in the cases for 2 minutes, then transfer to a wire rack to cool.

Make the icing by mixing the espresso coffee powder in a small bowl with the hot water until blended. Beat in the icing sugar and drizzle over the muffins.

For mocha cream muffins, make the muffins as above, omitting the raisins and marsala and replacing them with 50 g (2 oz) chopped white chocolate and 1 tablespoon cocoa powder. After baking, mix together 2 teaspoons caster sugar, ½ teaspoon ground cinnamon and ½ teaspoon cocoa powder and use to sprinkle generously over the muffins.

white chocolate raspberry cupcakes

Makes **16**
Preparation time **25 minutes**,
 plus cooling
Cooking time **12 minutes**

65 g (2½ oz) **lightly salted
 butter**, softened
40 g (1½ oz) **caster sugar**
65 g (2½ oz) **self-raising
 flour**
1 **egg**
40 g (1½ oz) **white chocolate**,
 chopped into small pieces

Topping
75 g (3 oz) **raspberries**
150 g (5 oz) **medium-fat soft
 cheese**
1 tablespoon **icing sugar**
chocolate curls, to decorate

Place 16 mini silicone muffin cases on a baking sheet.

Put the butter, sugar, flour and egg in a bowl and beat with a hand-held electric whisk until light and creamy. Stir in the chopped chocolate and divide among the cases.

Bake in a preheated oven, 180°C (350°F), Gas Mark 4, for 10–12 minutes, or until risen and just firm. Leave in the cases for 2 minutes, then transfer to a wire rack to cool completely.

Make the topping by putting the raspberries in a bowl and crushing with a fork until broken up. Put the soft cheese and icing sugar in a separate bowl and beat until smooth. Stir the crushed raspberries into the mixture until lightly combined but not completely blended. Spoon over the tops of the cakes and decorate with the chocolate curls.

For marshmallow cream cakes, make the cakes as above and leave to cool. Using a teaspoon, take a deep scoop out of the centre of the cakes and spread a little raspberry or strawberry jam in the bases. Lightly toast 16 marshmallows and push one into the centre of each cake. Whip 200 ml (7 fl oz) double cream with 1 tablespoon sifted icing sugar and put in a piping bag fitted with a 1 cm (½ inch) star nozzle. Pipe swirls up, around and over the marshmallows. Scatter with pink sugar sprinkles to decorate.

apricot cheesecake bites

Makes **16**
Preparation time **25 minutes**,
   plus cooling
Cooking time **25 minutes**

50 g (2 oz) **digestive biscuits**
15 g (½ oz) **unsalted butter**,
   melted
100 g (3½ oz) **caster sugar**
1 teaspoon **vanilla bean
   paste**
4 small **apricots**, stoned and
   quartered
200 g (7 oz) **cream cheese**
75 g (3 oz) **Greek yogurt**
1 **egg**, beaten

Place 16 mini silicone muffin cases on a baking sheet.

Put the biscuits in a polythene bag and crush with
a rolling pin until finely ground. Tip into a bowl and
mix with the melted butter. Divide among the cases,
pressing down firmly with the back of a teaspoon. Put
half the sugar in a saucepan with 6 tablespoons water
and the vanilla bean paste and heat until the sugar
dissolves. Add the apricots, cover and cook gently
for about 5 minutes until softened. Leave to cool.

Beat the remaining sugar with the cream cheese,
yogurt and egg until smooth. Spoon over the biscuit
bases.

Bake in a preheated oven, 180°C (350°F), Gas Mark 4,
for about 15 minutes, or until lightly set. Leave to cool
in the cases before transferring to a plate.

Drain the apricots from the syrup and place on the
cheesecakes. Cook the syrup left in the saucepan for
3–4 minutes until thick and syrupy. Spoon over the
apricots to serve.

For chocolate ginger cheesecakes, make the
biscuit base as above, using ginger biscuits instead
of digestives. Pack into the silicone cases. Finely
chop 2 pieces of preserved stem ginger in syrup. Beat
together 200 g (7 oz) cream cheese with 75 g (3 oz)
light muscovado sugar and 1 egg until smooth. Stir in
the chopped ginger and 100 g (3½ oz) melted plain
chocolate and spoon over the biscuit bases. Bake
as above. Leave to cool and serve dusted with
cocoa powder.

chocolate fudge cupcakes

Makes **16**
Preparation time **25 minutes**,
  plus cooling
Cooking time **12 minutes**

40 g (1½ oz) **cocoa powder**
100 ml (3½ fl oz) **boiling
  water**
50 g (2 oz) **lightly salted
  butter**, softened
125 g (4 oz) **light muscovado
  sugar**
1 **egg**
100 g (3½ oz) **self-raising
  flour**
150 g (5 oz) **raspberries**, to
  decorate

Frosting
75 g (3 oz) **plain dark
  chocolate**, chopped
1 tablespoon **milk**
25 g (1 oz) **lightly salted
  butter**
25 g (1 oz) **icing sugar**, sifted,
  plus extra for dusting

Place 16 mini silicone muffin cases on a baking sheet.

Whisk the cocoa powder with the boiling water in a
bowl. Leave to cool.

Beat together the butter and muscovado sugar in a
separate bowl until pale and creamy. Gradually beat in
the egg. Stir in the flour and then the cocoa mixture.
Divide among the cases.

Bake in a preheated oven, 180°C (350°F), Gas Mark 4,
for 8–10 minutes until risen and just firm to the touch.
Leave in the cases for 2 minutes, then transfer to a wire
rack to cool.

Make the frosting by putting the chocolate, milk and
butter in a small saucepan and heat gently until the
chocolate has melted to make a smooth sauce. Remove
from the heat. Sift the icing sugar into the chocolate
mixture and stir well. Use a palette knife to spread
the frosting over the cakes. Leave to cool completely.
Scatter with the raspberries and serve lightly dusted
with icing sugar.

For caramel pecan sauce, lightly toast and chop 50 g
(2 oz) pecan nuts. Put 100 ml (3½ fl oz) double cream
in a small saucepan with 125 g (4 oz) light muscovado
sugar and 50 g (2 oz) unsalted butter. Heat gently until
the sugar dissolves, then bring to the boil and cook for
about 5 minutes, stirring frequently until the syrup has
turned to a pale caramel colour. Don't let the mixture
bubble for too long or it will start to burn. Immerse the
base of the pan in cold water to prevent further cooking.
Stir in the nuts and serve as an alternative topping for
the fudge cakes.

mini minted cupcakes

Makes **50**
Preparation time **40 minutes**,
  plus cooling
Cooking time **14 minutes**

50 g (2 oz) **extra-strong
  mints** (about 1¼ tubes)
125 g (4 oz) **lightly salted
  butter**, softened
75 g (3 oz) **caster sugar**
2 **eggs**
125 g (4 oz) **self-raising flour**
½ teaspoon **baking powder**

To decorate
100 g (3½ oz) **plain dark
  chocolate**, chopped
25 g (1 oz) **milk chocolate**,
  chopped

Place 50 mini paper or foil cake (petit four) cases on a baking sheet.

Put the mints in a polythene bag and crush with a rolling pin until they are coarse crumbs. Tip the mints into a bowl and add all the remaining cake ingredients. Beat with a hand-held electric whisk for about a minute until light and creamy. Divide among the paper cases.

Bake in a preheated oven, 180°C (350°F), Gas Mark 4, for 12 minutes, or until risen and just firm to the touch. Transfer to a wire rack to cool.

Melt the plain and milk chocolate in separate bowls (see page 14). Put the melted milk chocolate in a paper piping bag and snip off the merest tip. Use a palette knife to spread the plain chocolate over the cakes. Use the milk chocolate to drizzle lines back and forth over the plain chocolate, or pipe little dots. Leave in a cool place to set before serving.

For mini mint fudge cakes, make the cake mixture as above, but substitute 15 g (½ oz) cocoa powder for 15 g (½ oz) of the flour. Bake as above. Melt 200 g (7 oz) white chocolate with 4 tablespoons milk, stirring until smooth. Stir in 150 g (5 oz) sifted icing sugar. Spread over the cooled cakes and dust with cocoa powder.

amaretti plum cakes

Makes **16**

Preparation time **15 minutes**, plus cooling

Cooking time **10 minutes**

40 g (1½ oz) **amaretti biscuits**

40 g (1½ oz) **light muscovado sugar**

65 g (2½ oz) **lightly salted butter**, softened

1 **egg**

65 g (2½ oz) **self-raising flour**

½ teaspoon **baking powder**

Icing

50 g (2 oz) **icing sugar**, sifted

2 teaspoons **lemon juice**

To decorate

4 **plums**, stoned and chopped

8 **unblanched almonds**, chopped

Place 16 mini silicone muffin cases on a baking sheet.

Put the biscuits in a polythene bag and crush with a rolling pin until finely ground. Tip into a bowl and add the sugar, butter and egg, then sift in the flour and baking powder. Beat with a hand-held electric whisk until smooth and creamy. Divide among the cases.

Bake in a preheated oven, 180°C (350°F), Gas Mark 4, for 10 minutes, or until risen and just firm. Leave in the cases for 2 minutes, then transfer to a wire rack to cool completely.

Make the icing by beating the icing sugar with the lemon juice to make a smooth paste. Spread a little over the cakes and sprinkle over pieces of the chopped plums and almonds. Drizzle a little more icing on top.

For apricot & ginger cakes, make the cakes as above, using crushed ginger nut biscuits instead of the amaretti and adding 1 finely chopped piece of preserved stem ginger in syrup. Use small apricots instead of the plums. After baking, drizzle the cakes with some of the stem ginger syrup instead of the icing.

maple butter pecan cupcakes

Makes **16**
Preparation time **20 minutes**,
plus cooling
Cooking time **12 minutes**

65 g (2½ oz) **lightly salted
butter**, softened
65 g (2½ oz) **caster sugar**
65 g (2½ oz) **self-raising
flour**, sifted
1 **egg**
40 g (1½ oz) **pecan nuts**,
finely chopped
16 **pecan nuts**, to decorate

Maple butter
100 g (3½ oz) **lightly salted
butter**, softened
½ teaspoon **vanilla bean
paste**
4 tablespoons **icing sugar**,
sifted
6 tablespoons **maple syrup**

Place 16 mini silicone muffin cases on a baking sheet.

Put the butter, sugar, flour and egg in a bowl and beat
with a hand-held electric whisk until light and creamy.
Stir in the chopped pecans and divide among the cases.

Bake in a preheated oven, 180°C (350°F), Gas Mark 4,
for 10–12 minutes, or until risen and just firm. Leave in
the cases for 2 minutes, then transfer to a wire rack to
cool completely.

Make the maple butter by beating together the butter,
vanilla bean paste and icing sugar until smooth and
creamy. Gradually blend in the maple syrup, beating
well until pale and fluffy. Place in a piping bag fitted
with a small star nozzle and pipe swirls on the top of
each cake. Decorate with pecan nuts.

For white chocolate & macadamia cupcakes,

make the sponge mixture as above, using chopped
macadamia nuts instead of the pecans and adding 25 g
(1 oz) chopped white chocolate and ½ teaspoon almond
extract. Bake and cool as above. Melt 50 g (2 oz) white
chocolate. Using a teaspoon, drizzle lines of chocolate
over the cooled cupcakes.

very fruity muffins

Makes **16**
Preparation time **10 minutes**
Cooking time **10 minutes**

50 g (2 oz) **redcurrants**
50 g (2 oz) **raspberries**
100 g (3½ oz) **self-raising flour**
1 teaspoon **baking powder**
50 g (2 oz) **caster sugar**
100 g (3½ oz) **strawberry** or **raspberry yogurt**
1 **egg**, beaten
2 tablespoons **vegetable oil**
1 teaspoon **vanilla extract**
icing sugar, for dusting (optional)

Pull the redcurrants from their stalks, if necessary, by running them between the tines of a fork. Mix with the raspberries and mash very lightly.

Place 16 mini silicone muffin cases on a baking sheet.

Sift the flour and baking powder into a bowl and stir in the sugar. Beat together the yogurt, egg, vegetable oil and vanilla extract and stir in the fruits. Add to the dry ingredients using a large metal spoon, stir the ingredients together until only just combined. Divide among the cases.

Bake in a preheated oven, 200°C (400°F), Gas Mark 6, for about 10 minutes until risen and firm. Leave in the cases for 2 minutes, then transfer to a wire rack to cool. Dust each muffin lightly with icing sugar.

For gooseberry & elderflower muffins, top and tail 100 g (3½ oz) gooseberries. Cut in half and put in a saucepan with 1 tablespoon water. Heat gently for 2–3 minutes until the berries start to soften. Remove from the heat and stir in 6 tablespoons elderflower cordial. Leave to cool. Complete the recipe as above, omitting the yogurt and vanilla extract and adding 25 g (1 oz) ground almonds and 1 teaspoon almond extract.

black forest bites

Makes **16**
Preparation time **20 minutes**,
    plus cooling
Cooking time **14 minutes**

65 g (2½ oz) **lightly salted
    butter**, softened
65 g (2½ oz) **light
    muscovado sugar**
1 **egg**
50 g (2 oz) **self-raising flour**
15 g (½ oz) **cocoa powder**
25 g (1 oz) **dried sour
    cherries**, chopped

Topping
100 g (3½ oz) **plain dark
    chocolate**, chopped
2 teaspoons **golden syrup**
150 ml (¼ pint) **double** or
    whipping cream
2 tablespoons **kirsch**
16 pitted canned **black
    cherries**
2 tablespoons **cherry** or **red
    fruit conserve**

Place 16 mini silicone muffin cases on a baking sheet.

Put the butter, sugar and egg in a bowl, sift in the flour and cocoa powder and beat with a hand-held electric whisk until light and creamy. Stir in the sour cherries and divide among the cases.

Bake in a preheated oven, 180°C (350°F), Gas Mark 4, for 10–12 minutes until risen and just firm. Leave in the cases for 2 minutes, then transfer to a wire rack to cool completely.

Make the topping by melting the chocolate (see page 14) and stirring in the syrup. Spoon over the chocolate sponges so the icing trickles down the sides. Whip the cream with the kirsch and spoon onto the cakes. Pat the cherries dry on kitchen paper and place on top of the cakes. If the conserve has a thick, jam-like consistency, heat in a small saucepan with 2 teaspoons water to soften, then cool slightly before drizzling over the cakes.

For glossy chocolate sauce, put 125 g (4 oz) light muscovado sugar in a small saucepan with 125 ml (4 fl oz) water. Heat gently, stirring until the sugar has dissolved, then bring to the boil and boil for 1 minute. Remove from the heat and stir in 200 g (7 oz) chopped plain chocolate and 25 g (1 oz) lightly salted butter. Leave the chocolate to melt, stirring occasionally and returning the pan to the heat if small pieces of chocolate remain. Serve as a warm sauce to go with the cakes.

mini cappuccino cakes

Makes **12**
Preparation time **30 minutes**
Cooking time **14 minutes**

3 teaspoons **instant coffee granules**
2 teaspoons boiling **water**
175 g (6 oz) **lightly salted butter**, softened, plus extra for greasing
175 g (6 oz) **light muscovado sugar**
2 tablespoons **cocoa powder**
175 g (6 oz) **self-raising flour**
½ teaspoon **baking powder**
3 **eggs**

To decorate
300 ml (½ pint) **double cream**
75 g (3 oz) **dark** or **white chocolate curls**

Grease the sections of a 12-hole deep muffin tin and line the bases with discs of greaseproof paper.

Dissolve the coffee in the boiling water. Put the remaining cake ingredients in a bowl and beat with a hand-held electric whisk until smooth. Stir in the dissolved coffee. Divide among the sections and spread the surfaces level.

Bake in a preheated oven, 180°C (350°F), Gas Mark 4, for 12–14 minutes until well risen and just firm to touch. Leave to cool in the tin for 5 minutes, then transfer to a wire rack and leave to cool completely.

Slice each cake in half horizontally. Whip the cream until softly peaking, then use to sandwich the cakes together in pairs and spoon the remainder on the tops. Sprinkle with the chocolate curls. These cakes are best eaten on the day they are made.

For mini chocolate sandwich cakes, make the cakes as above, omitting the coffee and replacing 25 g (1 oz) of the flour with 25 g (1 oz) cocoa powder. After baking, split the cakes and spread each with a thin layer of chocolate hazelnut spread and the whipped cream. Decorate the tops as above.

white chocolate & lavender cups

Makes **16**
Preparation time **30 minutes**,
  plus chilling
Cooking time **2 minutes**

125 g (4 oz) **white chocolate**,
  chopped
16 small **ratafia biscuits**
4 tablespoons **almond-
  flavoured liqueur** or **orange
  juice**
3 **lavender flowers**, plus extra
  to decorate
finely grated rind of ½ **orange**
3 tablespoons **caster sugar**
300 ml (½ pint) **double cream**
white chocolate shavings, to
  decorate

Melt the chocolate (see page 14). Place a teaspoonful into each of 16 mini silicone muffin cases and spread up the sides with the back of the teaspoon until evenly coated. Invert onto a baking sheet lined with nonstick baking paper. Chill for at least 1 hour or until set. Carefully peel away the silicone cases and place the chocolate cases upright.

Place a ratafia biscuit in each chocolate case and drizzle with the liqueur or orange juice.

Pull the lavender flowers from the stalks and put in a pestle with the orange rind and sugar. Pound the ingredients to bruise and mingle the flavours together. Turn into a bowl with the cream and whisk until the cream is only just holding its shape. Spoon into the cases and decorate with lavender flowers and white chocolate shavings.

Serve immediately or chill for up to 6 hours.

For white chocolate crunchies, melt 150 g (5 oz) white chocolate with 15 g (½ oz) unsalted butter until smooth. Leave until cool but not setting. Stir in 25 g (1 oz) chopped chocolate-coated honeycomb bar and 50 g (2 oz) diced shortbread biscuits. Pack into the silicone cases and scatter with white chocolate curls. Leave to set for several hours before removing from the cases.

cranberry mincemeat cupcakes

Makes **16**
Preparation time **30 minutes**,
plus soaking and cooling
Cooking time **12 minutes**

75 g (3 oz) **dried cranberries**
1 small **dessert apple**, peeled,
cored and diced
75 g (3 oz) **mixed dried fruit**
2 tablespoons **light
muscovado sugar**
½ teaspoon **ground mixed
spice**
2 tablespoons **sherry** or
ginger wine
65 g (2½ oz) **lightly salted
butter**, softened
65 g (2½ oz) **caster sugar**
65 g (2½ oz) **self-raising
flour**, sifted
1 **egg**

Frosting
2 **egg whites**
100 g (3½ oz) **icing sugar**,
sifted
¼ teaspoon **cream of tartar**

Put the dried cranberries, apple, mixed dried fruit, sugar, spice and sherry or ginger wine in a food processor and blend briefly until the ingredients are finely chopped but not puréed. (Or, chop the fruits as finely as possible before stirring in the other ingredients.) Stir well, then cover and leave to stand for several hours or overnight.

Place 16 mini silicone muffin cases on a baking sheet. Put the butter, sugar, flour and whole egg in a bowl and beat with a hand-held electric whisk until light and creamy. Divide among the cases. Bake in a preheated oven, 180°C (350°F), Gas Mark 4, for 10–12 minutes, or until risen and just firm. Leave to cool in the cases, then transfer to a wire rack. Scoop out a little from each centre and pile the mincemeat and juices on top.

Make the frosting by putting the egg whites, icing sugar and cream of tartar into a thoroughly clean heatproof bowl. Place the bowl over a pan of gently simmering water, making sure the base of the bowl does not rest in the water. Whisk using a hand-held electric whisk for about 5 minutes until beginning to thicken. Remove from the heat and whisk for a further 4–5 minutes for peaks. Pipe or spoon the frosting over the cupcakes, swirling with a palette knife to form soft peaks.

For amaretti & almond mincemeat, put 50 g (2 oz) plump dried apricots in a food processor with 1 small pear, peeled, cored and roughly chopped, 50 g (2 oz) raisins, 25 g (1 oz) blanched almonds, 1 tablespoon light muscovado sugar, ½ teaspoon ground cinnamon and 2 tablespoons amaretto liqueur. Blend until small pieces. Crumble 25 g (1 oz) amaretti or ratafia biscuits and blend briefly to mix. Use to replace the mincemeat.

chocolate caramel shortbreads

Makes **16**

Preparation time **20 minutes**,
plus cooling

Cooking time **17 minutes**

150 g (5 oz) **plain flour**
100 g (3½ oz) chilled **lightly salted butter**, diced
50 g (2 oz) **icing sugar**, sifted
1 **egg yolk**
½ teaspoon **vanilla extract**
75 g (3 oz) **plain dark** or **milk chocolate**, chopped
8 tablespoons **ready-made caramel sauce**

Place 16 mini silicone muffin cases on a baking sheet.

Put the flour and butter in a food processor and blend until the mixture resembles fine breadcrumbs, then lightly blend in the sugar. Add the egg yolk and vanilla extract and blend to make a soft dough. Shape the dough into 16 small balls and press a piece into the centre of each case.

Bake in a preheated oven, 200°C (400°F), Gas Mark 6, for 12–15 minutes until just starting to colour around the edges. Leave in the cases for 10 minutes, then transfer to a wire rack to cool.

Melt the chocolate (see page 14). Spoon a little caramel sauce into the centre of each shortbread and spread the melted chocolate on top.

For almond & polenta shortbreads, put 75 g (3 oz) caster sugar, 75 g (3 oz) ground almonds and 75 g (3 oz) polenta in a bowl. Add 75 g (3 oz) softened unsalted butter and the finely grated rind of 1 lemon. Beat well until the ingredients have combined to form a thick paste. Pack spoonfuls of the mixture into the cases, filling them to the tops. Bake as above and serve dusted with icing sugar.

red velvet mini cakes

Makes **16**
Preparation time **20 minutes**, plus cooling
Cooking time **10 minutes**

100 g (3½ oz) **self-raising flour**
2 teaspoons **cocoa powder**
50 g (2 oz) **golden caster sugar**
1 small raw **beetroot**, coarsely grated
2 tablespoons **vegetable oil**
1 **egg**
50 ml (2 fl oz) **buttermilk**
1 teaspoon **vinegar**
small **edible rose petals**, to decorate

Frosting
100 g (3½ oz) **cream cheese**
50 g (2 oz) **unsalted butter**, softened
1 teaspoon **vanilla bean paste**
100 g (3½ oz) **icing sugar**, sifted

Place 16 mini silicone muffin cases on a baking sheet.

Sift the flour and cocoa powder into a bowl. Stir in the sugar. Put the beetroot, oil and egg in a food processor or blender and blend to make a smooth purée. Briefly blend in the buttermilk and vinegar. Add to the dry ingredients. Using a large metal spoon, stir the ingredients together until combined. Divide among the cases.

Bake in a preheated oven, 180°C (350°F), Gas Mark 4, for 10 minutes, or until risen and just firm. Leave in the cases for 2 minutes, then transfer to a wire rack to cool completely.

Make the frosting by beating together the cream cheese, butter, vanilla bean paste and icing sugar until smooth and creamy. Place in a piping bag with a small star nozzle and pipe swirls on top of each cake. Decorate each with a rose petal.

For courgette & lime cupcakes, finely grate 75 g (3 oz) courgette, put in a small colander and sprinkle with 1 tablespoon salt. Leave to stand for 30 minutes, then rinse thoroughly in several changes of water to remove any traces of the salt. Make the cakes as above, replacing the cocoa powder with 1 tablespoon ground almonds, the beetroot with the courgette and the vinegar with the grated rind of 1 lime. Decorate with the frosting, replacing the vanilla bean paste with 1 tablespoon lime juice and omitting the rose petals.

gluten-free banoffi bites

Makes **24**
Preparation time **10 minutes**,
  plus cooling
Cooking time **12 minutes**

200 g (7 oz) **brown rice flour**
75 g (3 oz) **lightly salted
  butter**, softened
75 g (3 oz) **golden caster
  sugar**
2 teaspoons gluten-free
  baking powder
1 large **banana**, mashed
2 **eggs**
6 **toffees**, chopped
1 tablespoon **light
  muscovado sugar**
15 g (½ oz) **chewy banana
  slices** or **dried banana
  chips**, to decorate

Line 2 x 12-section mini muffin tins with paper cases.

Place the flour, butter, caster sugar, baking powder, banana and eggs in a bowl and beat with a hand-held electric whisk until smooth. Stir in the toffees. Divide among the cases and sprinkle over most of the muscovado sugar.

Bake in a preheated oven, 200°C (400°F), Gas Mark 6, for 10–12 minutes until just firm. Remove the cakes from the oven and transfer to a wire rack to cool.

Top with chewy banana slices or banana chips and sprinkle with the remaining sugar.

For walnut & muscovado butterflies, make the muffin mixture as above, replacing the toffees with 50 g (2 oz) finely chopped walnuts. Bake as above and leave to cool. Thoroughly beat 100 g (3½ oz) softened unsalted butter in a bowl with 125 g (4 oz) light muscovado sugar until smooth, pale and creamy. Cut a round from the centre top of each cake using a small sharp knife. Cut each round in half. Spoon or pipe the buttercream into the centres and position the halved rounds to resemble butterfly wings. Dust lightly with icing sugar.

chilli polenta cakes

Makes **16**
Preparation time **20 minutes**,
 plus cooling
Cooking time **10 minutes**

100 g (3½ oz) **polenta**
50 g (2 oz) **caster sugar**
½ teaspoon **baking powder**
40 g (1½ oz) **ground
 almonds**
2 tablespoons **olive oil**
2 **eggs**
juice of 1 **lime**
1 medium **red chilli**,
 deseeded and finely sliced

Icing
2 **limes**
100 g (3½ oz) **fondant icing
 sugar**

Place 16 mini silicone muffin cases on a baking sheet.

Put the polenta, sugar, baking powder and ground almonds in a bowl. Whisk the oil with the eggs, lime juice and half the chilli. Add to the dry ingredients. Using a large, metal spoon, stir the ingredients together and stir to make a smooth paste. Divide among the cases.

Bake in a preheated oven, 180°C (350°F), Gas Mark 4, for about 10 minutes until pale golden around the edges. Leave in the cases to cool.

Make the icing by using a citrus zester to pare thin curls of rind from the limes. Squeeze and measure 4 teaspoons of the juice. Beat the fondant icing sugar with the lime juice to give a consistency that thinly coats the back of the spoon, adding a dash more juice if necessary. Stir the lime rind into the icing. Place a little on each cake and spread down to the edges with a palette knife. Decorate each with one slice of chilli.

For fiery chocolate cupcakes, beat together 65 g (2½ oz) softened butter, 65 g (2½ oz) light muscovado sugar, 1 egg , 40 g (1½ oz) sifted self-raising flour, 25 g (1 oz) cocoa powder and 1 chopped medium deseeded red chilli until smooth and creamy. Divide among 16 mini silicone muffin cases on a baking sheet. Bake as above. Dissolve 2 tablespoons cocoa powder in 2 tablespoons boiling water to make a paste and leave to cool. Beat 75 g (3 oz) lightly salted softened butter with 100 g (3½ oz) sifted icing sugar until smooth. Beat in the cocoa mixture and pipe over the cakes. Decorate the top of each with a thin slice of chilli.

peanut caramel cupcakes

Makes **16**
Preparation time **20 minutes**,
  plus cooling
Cooking time **15 minutes**

65 g (2½ oz) **lightly salted
  butter**, softened
65 g (2½ oz) **light
  muscovado sugar**
65 g (2½ oz) **self-raising
  flour**
1 **egg**
50 g (1½ oz) **salted peanuts**,
  finely chopped, plus extra
  to decorate

Frosting
50 g (2 oz) **lightly salted
  butter**
100 g (3½ oz) **light
  muscovado sugar**
3 tablespoons **milk**
75 g (3 oz) **golden icing
  sugar**

Place 16 mini silicone muffin cases on a baking sheet.

Put the butter, sugar, flour and egg in a bowl and beat with a hand-held electric whisk until light and creamy. Stir in the chopped nuts. Divide among the cases.

Bake in a preheated oven, 180°C (350°F), Gas Mark 4, for 10–12 minutes, or until risen and just firm. Leave in the cases for 2 minutes then transfer to a wire rack to cool completely.

Make the frosting by heating the butter, sugar and milk in a saucepan until the sugar dissolves. Bring to the boil and boil for 1 minute until the mixture turns slightly syrupy. Remove from the heat and pour into a bowl. Sift the icing sugar into the bowl and beat until the mixture is smooth and fudge like.

Spread over the tops of the cakes with a palette knife and scatter with chopped peanuts.

For honey & pine nut cakes, toast and chop 100 g (3½ oz) pine nuts. Make the cakes as above, using half the pine nuts to replace the peanuts. Melt 25 g (1 oz) lightly salted butter in a small saucepan with 1½ tablespoons clear honey and 1 tablespoon light muscovado sugar. Bring to the boil and cook until syrupy. Remove from the heat and stir in 1 tablespoon lemon juice and the remaining pine nuts. Spoon over the cakes and serve warm.

chocolate tiramisu cups

Makes **16**
Preparation time **30 minutes**,
  plus chilling
Cooking time **2 minutes**

125 g (4 oz) **plain dark
  chocolate**, chopped
100 g (3½ oz) bought or
  homemade **vanilla sponge**,
  broken into small pieces
3 tablespoons **strong
  espresso coffee**, cooled
3 tablespoons **marsala,
  kahlua** or **Tia Maria**
small piece of **plain dark
  chocolate**, grated,
  to sprinkle

Frosting
250 g (8 oz) **mascarpone
  cheese**
4 tablespoons **icing sugar**,
  sifted
1 teaspoon **vanilla extract**
1 tablespoon **strong espresso
  coffee**, cooled
5 tablespoons **single cream**

Melt the chocolate (see page 14). Place a teaspoonful into each of 16 mini silicone muffin cases and spread up the sides with the back of the teaspoon until evenly coated. Invert onto a baking sheet lined with nonstick baking paper. Chill for at least 1 hour or until set. Peel away the silicone cases and place the chocolate cases upright.

Divide the pieces of vanilla sponge among the chocolate cases. Mix the coffee with the liqueur and spoon over the sponge.

Make the frosting by beating the mascarpone in a bowl with the icing sugar and vanilla extract. Beat in the coffee and cream until evenly combined. Place in a piping bag fitted with a small star nozzle and pipe swirls on top of each case. Scatter with grated chocolate and serve immediately or chill for up to 6 hours.

For mini trifle cups, make the chocolate cases as above. Split a 100 g (3½ oz) slice of Madeira cake in half and spread with 4 teaspoons raspberry or strawberry jam. Cut into small dice and place in the chocolate cups. Drizzle with 4 tablespoons sherry and scatter with 2 tablespoons chopped flaked almonds. Spoon 1 tablespoon custard into each cup. Whisk 150 ml (¼ pint) double cream with 1 tablespoon icing sugar until just peaking. Spoon or pipe over the cups and scatter with crushed toasted flaked almonds to decorate.

white chocolate coconut muffins

Makes **24**
Preparation time **15 minutes**
Cooking time **8 minutes**

150 g (5 oz) **self-raising flour**
½ teaspoon **bicarbonate
of soda**
75 g (3 oz) **golden caster
sugar**
50 g (2 oz) **sweetened
dessicated coconut**, plus 3
tablespoons for sprinkling
50 g (2 oz) **white chocolate
chips**
150 ml (¼ pint) **vanilla yogurt**
1 **egg**
4 tablespoons **sunflower oil**
3 tablespoons **strawberry jam**

Line 2 x 12-hole mini muffin tins with paper cases.

Sift the flour and bicarbonate of soda into a bowl and add the sugar, coconut and white chocolate chips.

Mix the yogurt, egg and sunflower oil together and add to the dry ingredients. Using a large metal spoon, stir the ingredients together until just combined. Divide among the cases.

Bake in a preheated oven, 190°C (375°F), Gas Mark 5, for 6–8 minutes until the muffins are well risen and firm. Transfer to a wire rack.

Brush with the strawberry jam while the muffins are still warm, and sprinkle over the remaining coconut.

For white chocolate strawberry muffins, chop 100 g (3½ oz) white chocolate and 100 g (3½ oz) dried strawberries into small pieces. Line a 12-hole muffin tin with small cupcake cases. Mix 225 g (7½ oz) self-raising flour and 1 teaspoon baking powder together in a bowl. Stir in 50 g (2 oz) caster sugar and the chopped ingredients. Mix 1 egg with 50 g (2 oz) melted lightly salted butter and 100 ml (3½ fl oz) milk. Add to the bowl and stir until only just mixed, adding a dash more milk if the mixture is dry. Divide among the cases and bake at 200°C (400°F), Gas Mark 6, for about 15 minutes until risen and pale golden. Serve dusted with icing sugar.

mini simnel cakes

Makes **12**
Preparation time **30 minutes**,
 plus soaking and cooling
Cooking time **30 minutes**

200 g (7 oz) **luxury mixed
 dried fruit**
3 tablespoons **brandy** or
 orange-flavoured liqueur
125 g (4 oz) **lightly salted
 butter**, softened
50 g (2 oz) **light muscovado
 sugar**
1 piece of **preserved stem
 ginger in syrup**, finely
 chopped, plus 2 tablespoons
 of the ginger syrup
2 **eggs**
150 g (5 oz) **self-raising flour**
½ teaspoon **baking powder**
½ teaspoon freshly grated
 nutmeg
325 g (11 oz) **white almond
 paste**
icing sugar, for dusting

Put the dried fruit and brandy or liqueur into a bowl and leave to soak for 1 hour. Line a 12-hole muffin tin with paper cases. Put the butter, sugar, ginger (and their syrup) and eggs in a bowl, sift in the flour, baking powder and nutmeg and beat with an electric whisk for 1 minute until smooth and creamy. Stir in the fruit and any liquid until mixed.

Roll 100 g (3½ oz) of the almond paste into a log shape, about 6 cm (2½ inches) long, and cut into 12 slices. Divide half the cake mixture between the cases and level with the back of a teaspoon. Place an almond paste slice over each. Cover with the remaining mixture. Bake in a preheated oven, 180°C (350°F), Gas Mark 4, for about 25 minutes until firm to the touch. Transfer to a wire rack to cool.

Roll out the remaining almond paste thinly on a work surface lightly dusted with icing sugar. Cut out 12 rounds with a 5 cm (2 inch) cutter. Brush the cakes with the ginger syrup and cover each with a paste round. Flatten a small piece of paste into a thin ribbon and roll up to make a rose. Place on top of the cake. Repeat for the remaining cakes. Heat under a medium grill on a baking sheet until lightly toasted, then dust with icing sugar.

For apricot & orange simnel cakes, make the cakes as above, replacing the nutmeg with the finely grated rind of 1 orange and the mixed dried fruit with 100 g (3½ oz) chopped dried apricots and 100 g (3½ oz) sultanas. After baking, cover with almond paste and brush with ginger syrup, scatter with flaked almonds and grill as above. Serve dusted with icing sugar.

mini christmas cakes

Makes **16**

Preparation time **40 minutes**, plus cooling

Cooking time **15 minutes**

50 g (2 oz) **lightly salted butter**, softened

50 g (2 oz) **dark muscovado sugar**

1 **egg**

65 g (2½ oz) **self-raising flour**

½ teaspoon **ground mixed spice**

¼ teaspoon **baking powder**

65 g (2½ oz) **mixed dried fruit**

15 g (½ oz) **Brazil nuts**, chopped

2 tablespoons **brandy** or **orange-flavoured liqueur**

2 tablespoons **smooth apricot jam**

1 teaspoon **hot water**

250 g (8 oz) **marzipan**

icing sugar, for dusting

150 g (5 oz) **royal icing sugar**, sifted

edible silver balls, to decorate

Place 16 mini silicone muffin cases on a baking sheet.

Put the butter, sugar and egg in a bowl, sift in the flour, mixed spice and baking powder and beat with a hand-held electric whisk until light and creamy. Beat in the dried fruit and nuts. Divide among the cases.

Bake in a preheated oven, 180°C (350°F), Gas Mark 4, for 15 minutes, or until risen and just firm. Leave in the cases for 2 minutes then transfer to a wire rack to cool completely.

Using a skewer or cocktail stick, pierce holes over the tops of the cakes and spoon over the brandy or orange liqueur. Store in an airtight container for up to 1 week.

Mix the apricot jam with the hot water and brush over the tops of the cakes. Thinly roll out the marzipan on a surface dusted with icing sugar and cut out 4cm (1¾ inch) rounds using a small cutter, re-rolling the trimmings to make more. Press onto tops of the cakes.

Beat the royal icing sugar in a bowl with enough cold water to make a softly peaking consistency. Swirl a little over the cakes and decorate with silver balls.

For Christmas tree cakes, make the cakes as above and cover with marzipan. Thinly roll out 100 g (3½ oz) green ready-to-roll icing on a surface dusted with icing sugar and cut out 16 simple Christmas tree shapes using a small cutter. Transfer to a baking paper lined tray for 2–3 hours to firm up. Spread the cakes with royal icing as above and gently position a tree on top of each. Decorate with garlands of red writing icing, pushing silver balls into the piping to secure.

biscuits & cookies

viennese whirls

Makes **16**
Preparation time **15 minutes**,
plus cooling
Cooking time **20 minutes**

200 g (7 oz) **unsalted butter**,
softened
50 g (2 oz) **caster sugar**
250 g (8 oz) **plain flour**, sifted
1 teaspoon **vanilla extract**
3 tablespoons **raspberry** or
strawberry jam
vanilla sugar (see page 168),
for sprinkling

Place 16 mini silicone muffin cases on a baking sheet.

Beat together the butter and sugar until very pale and
creamy. Beat in the flour and vanilla extract until smooth.
Place in a piping bag fitted with a 1 cm (½ inch) star
nozzle. Pipe a little mixture into the base of each case.
Pipe a ring of the mixture on top to create nest shapes.

Bake in a preheated oven, 180°C (350°F), Gas Mark 4,
for 15–20 minutes until pale golden. Leave in the cases
for 5 minutes, then transfer to a wire rack. Impress holes
into the centres of the nests if they have expanded
during cooking. Leave to cool.

Place a little jam in the centre of each nest and sprinkle
vanilla sugar over the edges.

For chocolate thumbprint biscuits, make the biscuit
mixture as above, replacing 25 g (1 oz) of the flour with
25 g (1 oz) cocoa powder. Spoon the mixture into the
cases and push a hole into the centre of each, using
your thumb. Bake as above and leave to cool. Put 5
tablespoons chocolate hazelnut spread in a piping bag
fitted with a small star nozzle and pipe a swirl into the
centre of each.

florentines

Makes **48**
Preparation time **30 minutes**,
  plus cooling and setting
Cooking time about **20
  minutes**

150 g (5 oz) **lightly salted
  butter**, plus extra for
  greasing
175 g (6 oz) **caster sugar**
4 tablespoons **double cream**
75 g (3 oz) **mixed candied
  peel**, chopped
50 g (2 oz) **glacé cherries**,
  chopped
50 g (2 oz) **flaked almonds**
40 g (1½ oz) **dried
  cranberries**
25 g (1 oz) **pine nuts**
50 g (2 oz) **plain flour**, sifted
150 g (5 oz) **plain dark
  chocolate**
150 g (5 oz) **white chocolate**

Grease 2 large baking sheets and line with nonstick baking paper. Heat the butter and sugar gently in a pan until the butter has melted. Increase the heat and bring to the boil. Immediately remove the pan from the heat, add the cream, mixed peel, cherries, almonds, cranberries, pine nuts and flour. Stir well to combine.

Drop 12 heaped teaspoonfuls (a quarter of the mixture) onto each of the baking sheets, leaving a 5 cm (2 inch) gap between each for spreading. Bake in a preheated oven, 180°C (350°F), Gas Mark 4, for 7 minutes. Remove the baking sheets from the oven.

Use a 7 cm (3 inch) cookie cutter to drag the edges of the biscuits carefully into neat rounds so that they are about 5 cm (2 inches) across. Bake for a further 3–4 minutes until golden around the edges. Remove from the oven and leave for 2 minutes. Use a palette knife to transfer the biscuits to baking paper on a work surface and leave to cool. Repeat with the remaining mixture. Melt the plain dark and white chocolate in separate bowls (see page 14). Spoon the chocolate into separate piping bags, drizzle on top of the biscuits and leave to set.

For pistachio & white chocolate florentines, steep 50 g (2 oz) shelled pistachio nuts in boiling water for 1 minute. Drain and rub between several sheets of kitchen paper to remove the skins. Peel away any remaining skins and chop the nuts into small pieces. Make the Florentines as above, replacing the pine nuts with the pistachio nuts and the cranberries with 25 g (1 oz) raisins. Melt 250 g (8 oz) chopped white chocolate and roll the edges of the Florentines in the chocolate. Transfer to a sheet of nonstick baking paper until set.

chilli & cardamom morsels

Makes **24**
Preparation time **15 minutes**
Cooking time **12 minutes**

10 **cardamom pods**
2 **egg whites**
2 teaspoons **cornflour**
½ teaspoon **hot chilli powder**
125 g (4 oz) **caster sugar**
75 g (3 oz) **ground almonds**

Grease and line a large baking sheet with nonstick baking paper.

Crush the cardamom pods using a pestle and mortar to release the seeds. Remove the shells and crush the seeds until fairly finely ground.

Whisk the egg whites in a thoroughly clean bowl until peaking. Sift the cornflour and chilli powder into the bowl and sprinkle in the crushed cardamom. Add the sugar and ground almonds and gently fold the ingredients together to make a sticky paste.

Place in a piping bag fitted with a 1 cm (½ inch) plain nozzle and pipe fingers, 5 cm (2 inches) long, onto the baking sheet, spacing them slightly apart.

Bake in a preheated oven, 180°C (350°F), Gas Mark 4, for 10–12 minutes until crisp and pale golden. Transfer to a wire rack to cool.

For hazelnut & orange fingers, blend 75 g (3 oz) blanched hazelnuts in a food processor or blender until ground. Make the fingers as above, omitting the spices and adding the finely grated rind of 1 small orange with the caster sugar and adding the hazelnuts instead of the ground almonds.

mini orange shortbreads

Makes about **80**
Preparation time **10 minutes**,
  plus cooling
Cooking time **12 minutes**

175 g (6 oz) chilled **unsalted
  butter**, diced, plus extra for
  greasing
250 g (8 oz) **plain flour**, sifted,
  plus extra for dusting
grated rind of 1 **orange**
½ teaspoon **ground mixed
  spice**
75 g (3 oz) **caster sugar**
2 teaspoons cold **water**

To serve
2 teaspoons **icing sugar**
1 teaspoon **cocoa powder**

Grease and line 2 large baking sheets with nonstick baking paper.

Put the flour and butter in a food processor and blend until the mixture resembles fine breadcrumbs. Stir in the remaining ingredients with the measurement water and mix to form a dough.

Roll out the dough on a lightly floured surface to 2.5 mm (⅛ inch) thick. Cut out about 80 rounds using a 1.5 cm (¾ inch) plain cutter, and place on the baking sheets.

Bake in a preheated oven, 200°C (400°F), Gas Mark 6, for 10–12 minutes until golden. Carefully transfer to a wire rack to cool.

Mix together the icing sugar and cocoa powder and dust a little over the shortbreads before serving.

For lemon & cardamom shortbreads, crush 10 cardamom pods using a pestle and mortar to release the seeds. Remove the shells and crush the seeds a little more until ground. Make the shortbread as above, replacing the orange rind and mixed spice with the finely grated rind of 1 lemon and the ground cardamom and using lemon juice to replace the water. Serve dusted with icing sugar.

vanilla & rosewater sables

Makes about **20**
Preparation time **30 minutes**,
  plus chilling and cooling
Cooking time **8 minutes**

275 g (9 oz) **plain flour**, sifted,
  plus extra for dusting
200 g (7 oz) **chilled unsalted
  butter**, diced, plus extra
  for greasing
100 g (3½ oz) **icing sugar**,
  sifted
2 **egg yolks**
2 teaspoons **vanilla bean
  paste**

Buttercream
50 g (2 oz) **unsalted butter**,
  softened
75 g (3 oz) **icing sugar**, sifted,
  plus extra for dusting
1 teaspoon **boiling water**
few drops of **pink food
  colouring**
1–2 teaspoons **rosewater**

Grease 2 baking sheets. Put the flour and butter in a food processor and blend until the mixture resembles breadcrumbs. Add the sugar, egg yolks and vanilla bean paste and blend to make a smooth dough. Wrap in clingfilm and chill for an hour.

Roll out half the dough on a lightly floured surface to about 2.5 mm (⅛ inch) thick, and cut out heart shapes using a 4 cm (1¾ inch) heart-shaped cutter. Space slightly apart on a baking sheet. Roll out the remaining dough and shape more hearts. Put on the second baking sheet and reroll the trimmings for extra. Bake in a preheated oven, 200°C (400°F), Gas Mark 6, for about 8 minutes, or until just beginning to turn golden around the edges. Transfer to a wire rack to cool.

Make the buttercream by beating together the butter and icing sugar in a bowl until smooth. Add the boiling water, the pink food colouring and enough of the rosewater to give a delicate flavour, then beat until pale and creamy. Use the buttercream to sandwich the biscuits together. Serve lightly dusted with icing sugar.

For ginger & nougat sables, make the biscuits as above, using 2 teaspoons ground ginger instead of the vanilla bean paste, and golden icing sugar to replace the white sugar. Cut out 4 cm (1¾ inch) circles instead of hearts. For the filling, put 75 g (3 oz) pink or white nougat in a heatproof bowl with 1 tablespoon milk and rest over a bowl of simmering water until the nougat has melted. Remove from the heat and cool. In a separate bowl, whisk together 25 g (1 oz) softened butter and 25 g (1 oz) sifted icing sugar until smooth. Stir in the nougat and use to sandwich the biscuits together.

triple chocolate pretzels

Makes **40**
Preparation time **30 minutes**,
  plus proving and setting
Cooking time **8 minutes**

15 g (½ oz) **butter**, melted
225 g (7½ oz) **strong white
  bread flour**, plus extra for
  dusting
1 teaspoon **fast-action dried
  yeast**
2 teaspoons **caster sugar**
large pinch of **salt**
100 ml (3½ fl oz) warm **water**
75 g (3 oz) each **plain dark,
  white** and **milk chocolate**,
  broken into pieces

Glaze
2 tablespoons **water**
½ teaspoon **salt**

Grease 2 large baking sheets. Put the flour, yeast, sugar and salt into a bowl. Add the melted butter or oil and gradually mix in the measurement water until you have a smooth dough. Knead the dough for 5 minutes on a lightly floured surface until smooth and elastic.

Cut the dough into quarters, then cut each quarter into 10 smaller pieces. Shape each piece into a thin rope about 20 cm (8 inches) long. Bend the rope in a wide arc, then bring one of the ends round in a loop and secure about halfway along. Do the same with the other end, looping it across the first. Transfer the pretzels to the baking sheets. Cover with lightly oiled clingfilm and leave in a warm place for 30 minutes until well risen.

Mix the glaze water and salt in a bowl until the salt has dissolved and brush over the pretzels. Bake in a preheated oven, 200°C (400°F), Gas Mark 6, for 6–8 minutes until golden. Transfer to a wire rack to cool. Melt the dark, white and milk chocolates in separate heatproof bowls (see page 14). Drizzle lines of dark chocolate over the pretzels. Leave to set and repeat with the white and milk chocolate. Store in an airtight container for 2 days.

For glossy chocolate dip, put 150 g (5 oz) light muscovado sugar in a saucepan with 100 ml (3½ fl oz) water and heat gently until the sugar dissolves. Bring to the boil and boil for 4 minutes until syrupy. Remove from the heat and add 2 tablespoons water. Return to the heat and cook, stirring until smooth. Add 50 g (2 oz) unsalted butter and 200 g (7 oz) chopped plain dark chocolate. Heat gently, stirring, until the chocolate has melted. Stir in 100 ml (3½ fl oz) double cream and pour into a bowl. Serve with the pretzels for dipping.

vanilla fudge nuggets

Makes **16**
Preparation time **15 minutes**,
 plus chilling
Cooking time **20 minutes**

75 g (3 oz) **unsalted butter**,
 softened
75 g (3 oz) **golden caster
 sugar**
1 **egg yolk**, plus 1 tablespoon
 egg white
150 g (5 oz) **self-raising flour**,
 sifted, plus extra for dusting
8 pieces of **soft vanilla fudge**,
 cut in half
icing sugar, for dusting

Place 16 mini silicone muffin cases on a baking sheet.

Put the butter and sugar in a bowl and beat until pale
and fluffy. Beat in the egg yolk and white, then add the
flour and mix to make a firm dough. Knead into a ball,
wrap in clingfilm and chill for at least 30 minutes.

Divide the dough in half and press half the dough
into the cases. Push a piece of fudge down into the
centre of each case. Divide the remaining dough into
16 pieces. Roll each piece into a ball using lightly
floured hands and flatten into a round roughly 5 cm
(2 inches) in diameter. Push a circle of dough into
each case, covering the fudge, and press it down
firmly around the edges.

Bake in a preheated oven, 190°C (375°F), Gas Mark 5,
for 15–20 minutes, or until slightly risen. Leave in the
cases for 5 minutes, then transfer to a wire rack to
cool. Serve lightly dusted with icing sugar.

For double-choc nuggets, make the dough as above,
replacing 25 g (1 oz) of the flour with 25 g (1 oz) cocoa
powder. Assemble the biscuits, replacing the pieces
of fudge with squares of plain or milk chocolate. After
baking, dust lightly with cocoa powder.

white chocolate drops

Makes **20**
Preparation time **10 minutes**,
  plus chilling and cooling
Cooking time **20 minutes**

50 g (2 oz) **butter**, softened,
  plus extra for greasing
50 g (2 oz) **white vegetable
  fat**, softened
50 g (2 oz) **caster sugar**
1 **egg yolk**
200 g (7 oz) **brown rice flour**,
  plus extra for dusting
1 tablespoon **ground
  almonds**
50 g (2 oz) **white chocolate**,
  grated
2 teaspoons **icing sugar**, for
  dusting

Grease and line 2 baking sheets with nonstick
baking paper.

Put the fats and sugar in a bowl and beat together,
then beat in the egg yolk followed by the remaining
ingredients. Form the dough into a ball, wrap in clingfilm
and chill for 1 hour.

Knead the dough on a lightly floured surface to soften
it, then divide into 20 balls. Place the balls on the baking
sheets and flatten them slightly with a fork.

Bake in a preheated oven, 180°C (350°F), Gas Mark
4, for about 20 minutes until golden. Transfer to a wire
rack to cool. Dust over a little icing sugar before serving.

For dark chocolate drops, beat together 125 g
(4 oz) softened lightly salted butter, 125 g (4 oz) light
muscovado sugar, 1 egg, 1 teaspoon vanilla extract,
125 g (4 oz) sifted self-raising flour and 25 g (1 oz)
cocoa powder. Stir in 100 g (3½ oz) chopped plain dark
or milk chocolate. Take teaspoonfuls of the mixture and
space slightly apart on 2 greased baking sheets. Bake
at 200°C (400°F), Gas Mark 6 for 10 minutes until
beginning to darken around the edges. Transfer to a
wire rack to cool. Serve dusted with cocoa powder.

pistachio biscotti

Makes about **24**
Preparation time **15 minutes**,
  plus cooling
Cooking time **30 minutes**

25 g (1 oz) **lightly salted
  butter**, softened, plus extra
  for greasing
50 g (2 oz) **caster sugar**
finely grated **rind** of 1 **lemon**
125 g (4 oz) **self-raising flour**
½ teaspoon **baking powder**
1 **egg yolk**, plus 1 tablespoon
  egg white
65 g (2½ oz) **shelled
  pistachio nuts**, skinned
  and roughly chopped (see
  page 70)

Grease a baking sheet.

Put the butter, sugar and lemon rind in a bowl and beat together, then sift in the flour and baking powder. Add the egg yolk, egg white and pistachios and mix to a soft dough.

Divide the dough into 2 pieces and shape each roughly into a sausage measuring about 15 cm (6 inches) long. Space the 2 pieces well apart on the baking sheet and flatten each to a depth of 1 cm (½ inch).

Bake in a preheated oven, 160°C (325°F), Gas Mark 3, for 20 minutes until risen and turning pale golden. Remove from the oven and leave to cool for 10 minutes, leaving the oven on. Using a serrated knife, cut the biscuits across into 1 cm (½ inch) thick slices. Return to the baking sheet, cut sides face up and bake for a further 10 minutes to crisp up. Transfer to a wire rack to cool. Store in an airtight container for up to 1 week.

For walnut oat cookies, mix together 50 g (2 oz) sifted self-raising flour, 50 g (2 oz) porridge oats, 40 g (1½ oz) chopped walnuts and ¼ teaspoon bicarbonate of soda in a bowl. Put 50 g (2 oz) lightly salted butter, 50 g (2 oz) golden caster sugar and 1 tablespoon golden syrup in a small saucepan. Heat gently until the butter has melted. Add to the oat mixture and stir well to mix. Roll teaspoonfuls of the mixture into small balls and space well apart on a greased baking sheet. Bake as above for about 15 minutes until pale golden. Transfer to a wire rack to cool.

birthday bundles

Makes **12 cookies** (4 bundles)
Preparation time **50 minutes**,
  plus chilling and setting
Cooking time **18 minutes**

200 g (7 oz) chilled **unsalted
  butter, diced, plus extra for
  greasing**
275 g (9 oz) **plain flour,
  sifted, plus extra for
  dusting**
100 g (3½ oz) **light
  muscovado sugar**
2 teaspoons **ground ginger**
2 **egg yolks**
2 teaspoons **vanilla bean
  paste**

To decorate
150 g (5 oz) **icing sugar,
  sifted**
5–6 teaspoons **lemon** or **lime
  juice**
**different-coloured sugar
  sprinkles**
fine ribbon, in 2 colours, for
  wrapping bundles

Grease and line a baking sheet with nonstick baking paper. Put the flour and butter in a food processor and blend until the mixture resembles breadcrumbs. Add the sugar, ground ginger, egg yolks and vanilla bean paste and blend to make a smooth dough. Wrap in clingfilm and chill for at least 1 hour.

Roll out the dough on a lightly floured surface to between 2.5 mm (⅛ inch) and 5 mm (¼ inch) thick and transfer to the baking sheet. Cut off the rough edges, but leave them in position to keep the dough in place. Cut out 12 x 5 cm (2 inches) squares from the dough. Bake in a preheated oven, 180°C (350°F), Gas Mark 4, for 16–18 minutes or until risen slightly and beginning to darken around the edges. Recut the marked lines and transfer the cookies to a wire rack to cool. Beat the icing sugar in a bowl with enough of the lemon or lime juice to give a consistency that thickly covers the back of the spoon. Using a teaspoon, drizzle wavy lines of citrus glaze over the top of a cookie, then brush more around the sides.

Scatter with sugar sprinkles, tipping off the excess, then dip the sides in sugar sprinkles. Transfer the cookie to the baking paper. Repeat with the remaining cookies, then leave in a cool place to set for 2 hours. Stack the cookies in little bundles and tie with ribbon.

For ginger cream biscuits, roll out the gingerbread dough as above and cut out rounds using a 6 cm (2½ inch) round cutter. Bake as above. Beat together 75 g (3 oz) softened unsalted butter with 100 g (3½ oz) icing sugar and ½ teaspoon vanilla extract until smooth and creamy. Use to sandwich the biscuits together.

pink champagne cocktails

Makes **16**

Preparation time **45 minutes**, plus cooling

Cooking time **15 minutes**

200 g (7 oz) chilled **unsalted butter**, diced, plus extra for greasing

275 g (9 oz) **plain flour**, plus extra for dusting

100 g (3½ oz) **icing sugar**

2 **egg yolks**

2 teaspoons **vanilla bean paste**

flour, for dusting

a few drops of **pink liquid** or **paste food colouring**

sugar sprinkles

pink-tinted silver balls

Buttercream

1 cup confectioners' sugar, sifted

1/3 cup unsalted butter, softened

Put the flour and butter in a food processor and blend until the mixture resembles bread crumbs. Add the sugar, egg yolks, and vanilla bean paste and blend until the mixture comes together to form a smooth dough. Wrap in plastic wrap and chill for at least 1 hour.

Trace and cut out a cocktail glass shape from a picture, about 10 x 8 cm (4 x 3¼ inches), for use as a template. Grease 2 baking sheets. Roll out the cookie dough on a lightly floured surface. Lay the template over the dough and, using a small, sharp knife or scalpel, cut around it. Place on the baking sheets, spacing them slightly apart, and reroll the trimmings to make 16 in all.

Bake in a preheated oven, 180°C (350°F), Gas Mark 4, for 15 minutes, or until pale golden. Transfer to a wire rack to cool. Beat the food colouring into the buttercream and put half in a piping bag fitted with a fine plain nozzle. Spread a little frosting across the centre of the cookies so they look like half-filled glasses. Pipe an outline of frosting around the cookie edges. Scatter the glass cavity area with sugar sprinkles. Pipe frosting dots for the bubbles and sprinkle with the pink-tinted silver balls.

For pumpkin-face cookies, make the dough as above, using light muscovado sugar instead of caster, adding 1 teaspoon ground mixed spice and ½ teaspoon ground ginger. Roll out and cut out pumpkin shapes using a cookie cutter or by hand. Cut out small triangles for eyes and nose and a small mouth from each. Bake as above. Put 100 g (3½ oz) royal icing sugar in a bowl and beat in enough water to make a smooth icing that thickly coats the back of the spoon. Add a few drops of orange food colouring. Use to pipe outlines around the cookies.

shooting stars

Makes **24**

Preparation time **1 hour**, plus
chilling, cooling and setting

Cooking time **15 minutes**

200 g (7 oz) chilled **unsalted
butter**, diced, plus extra for
greasing

275 g (9 oz) **plain flour**, sifted,
plus extra for dusting

100 g (3½ oz) **light
muscovado sugar**

2 teaspoons **ground ginger**

2 **egg yolks**

2 **teaspoons vanilla bean
paste**

To decorate

200g (7oz) **royal icing sugar**

a few drops each of **orange**
and **yellow liquid** or **paste
food colourings**

edible **gold food colouring**

Grease 2 baking sheets. Put the flour and butter in a
food processor and blend until the mixture resembles
breadcrumbs. Add the sugar, ground ginger, egg yolks
and vanilla bean paste and blend to make a smooth
dough. Wrap in clingfilm and chill for at least 1 hour.

Roll out the dough on a lightly floured surface and cut
out shooting star-shaped cookies using a cookie cutter.
Place on the baking sheets, spacing them slightly apart,
and reroll the trimmings to make 24 in total. Bake in
a preheated oven, 180°C (350°F), Gas Mark 4, for 15
minutes or until the dough has risen slightly and is
beginning to darken. Using a spatula, transfer to a
wire rack to cool.

Put the royal icing sugar in a bowl and beat in enough
cold water, about 5 teaspoons, to make a thick but
smooth paste. Divide the royal icing between 2 bowls
and colour 1 orange and 1 yellow. Place in 2 separate
piping bags fitted with fine nozzles (or use paper piping
bags and snip off the tips). Pipe star-shaped outlines
and broken lines of piping on the tails of the stars. Leave
in a cool place to set for about 30 minutes. Use the gold
food colouring to paint highlights over the cookies.

For festive tree biscuits, roll out the spiced dough as
above and cut out Christmas tree shapes with a cutter.
Place on the baking sheets. Lightly toast 50 g (2 oz)
pine nuts and arrange in rows over the biscuits, pressing
them in gently. Bake as above. Put 200 g (7 oz) royal
icing sugar in a bowl and beat in enough water to make
a smooth icing that thickly coats the back of the spoon.
Drizzle the icing over the biscuits with a teaspoon.

shoes & bags

Makes about **20**
Preparation time **1¼ hours**,
  plus cooling and setting
Cooking time **15 minutes**

200 g (7 oz) chilled **unsalted
  butter**, diced, plus extra for
  greasing
275 g (9 oz) **plain flour**, plus
  extra for dusting
100 g (3½ oz) **icing sugar**
2 **egg yolks**
2 teaspoons **vanilla bean
  paste**
1 quantity **Royal Icing** (see
  page 15)
few drops of **pink** or **lilac
  liquid** or **paste food
  colouring**
selection of **tiny pink sweets**
  or **cake decorations**

Grease 2 baking sheets. Cut out simple pictures of
a shoe and a bag from a magazine. Put the flour and
butter in a food processor and blend until it resembles
breadcrumbs. Add the sugar, egg yolks and vanilla bean
paste and blend to a smooth dough. Wrap in clingfilm
and chill for at least 1 hour. Roll out the dough on a
lightly floured surface. Lay the templates over the dough
and, using a small, sharp knife cut around them. Place
on the baking sheets, spaced slightly apart. Reroll the
trimmings for extras. Bake in a preheated oven, 180°C
(350°F), Gas Mark 4, for 15 minutes, or until pale golden.
Transfer to a wire rack to cool. Place a little icing in a
piping bag fitted with a fine plain nozzle. Pipe an outline
around each cookie, slightly away from the edges,
adding lines of piping for heels, soles and boot tops.

Divide the remaining icing between 2 bowls. Add the
food colouring to 1 bowl. Stir a few drops of water into
each bowl until the icing forms a flat surface when
left to stand for 15 seconds. Use a small teaspoon
to drizzle a little of the coloured icing onto a cookie,
easing it to the edges and into the corners. Repeat on
the remaining cookies so some are covered in coloured
icing, while others are white. Before the icing dries,
gently press the sweets or decorations into them. Leave
in a cool place for about 1 hour. Use the remaining
icing in the bag to pipe decorations such as flowers and
borders on the purses and at the tops of the shoes.

For pink heart biscuits, make the biscuit dough as
above and cut out heart shapes. Bake as above. Beat
a few drops of pink food colouring into the icing. Pipe
outlines around the edges of the biscuits and decorate
the centres.

baby shower cookies

Makes **20**
Preparation time **1 hour**, plus
  cooling and setting
Cooking time **15 minutes**

butter, for greasing
1 quantity **Vanilla Cookie
  Dough**, chilled (see page
  230)
flour, for dusting
1 quantity **Royal Icing** (see
  page 15)
5 **pink jelly beans**, halved
  lengthwise
75 g (3 oz) **pale blue, pink** or
  yellow ready-to-roll icing
10 small **blue, pink** or **yellow
  ribbon bows**

Copy the bootie and bottle shapes opposite to make simple templates. Grease 2 baking sheets. Roll out the cookie dough thinly on a lightly floured surface. Lay the templates over the dough and, using a small, sharp knife or scalpel, cut around them. Place on the baking sheets, spacing them slightly apart, and reroll the trimmings to make 20 in all.

Bake in a preheated oven, 180°C (350°F), Gas Mark 4, for 15 minutes, or until pale golden. Transfer to a wire rack to cool. Place a little of the royal icing in a piping bag fitted with a fine plain nozzle. Add a few drops of water to the remaining icing until the icing forms a flat surface when left to stand for 15 seconds.

Pipe a line of icing around the edges of the cookies. Pipe a line of circles across the ankles of the booties and a diagonal line of piping across the centre of the bottles. Using a small teaspoon, drizzle a little of the thinned icing onto the lower part of the bottles, spreading it to the edges with the back of a teaspoon and easing it into the corners with a cocktail stick. Spread the icing onto the bootie-shaped cookies in the same way, easing it around the piping across the ankles.

Secure a jelly-bean half, cut side down, to the top of each bottle with a little icing. Shape a little band of ready-to-roll icing and secure around the neck of the bottles. Leave for 30 minutes leave for 30 minutes. Pipe white decorative lines and secure bows with dots of icing to finish the booties and pipe ready-to-use icing on the bottles. Leave to set again for 30 minutes.

scrabble cookies

Makes **30**
Preparation time **35 minutes**
Cooking time **5 minutes**, plus
   chilling and cooling

75 g (3 oz) **unsalted butter**,
   softened, plus extra for
   greasing
75 g (3 oz) **caster sugar**
1 **egg**
½ teaspoon **vanilla extract**
250 g (8 oz) **plain flour**, sifted,
   plus extra for dusting

To decorate
375 g (12 oz) **ready-to-roll
   icing**
icing sugar, for dusting
2–3 tablespoons **apricot jam**,
   sieved
1 small tube of **coloured
   writing icing**

Grease and line 2 baking sheets with nonstick baking paper. Beat together the butter and sugar until pale and fluffy. Gradually beat in the egg and vanilla extract adding a little flour to prevent the mixture curdling. Add the flour and fold in to make a stiff dough. Wrap in clingfilm and refrigerate for 20 minutes.

Roll out the dough on a lightly floured surface to 2.5 mm (⅛ inch) thick. Cut out about 30 rounds, using a 4–5 cm (1½–2 inch) diameter cookie cutter, rerolling the trimmings as necessary. Place on the baking sheets.

Bake in a preheated oven, 180°C (350°F), Gas Mark 4, for 5 minutes, or until a pale golden colour. Transfer to a wire rack and leave to cool. Roll out the white icing on a sugar-dusted surface until 2.5 mm (⅛ inch) thick. Using the same cutter as before, dusted this time with a little icing sugar, cut out the same number of circles. Using a clean paintbrush, paint a little of the sieved jam on each cookie to ensure that the icing will stick, place the icing shapes on the cookies and press down lightly. Using the coloured writing icing, write a letter on each cookie to spell out the name or message.

For homemade ready-to-roll icing, put 1 tablespoon egg white in a bowl with 1 tablespoon liquid glucose and 100 g (3½ oz) sifted icing sugar and beat to a smooth paste. Gradually work in a further 150 g (5 oz) icing sugar, stirring well until the mixture is very firm. Turn out onto the work surface and knead to a smooth paste, which should be firm and rollable, not sticky. Work in a little more icing sugar if necessary. Wrap tightly in several thicknesses of clingfilm and store until ready.

slices &
traybakes

chocolate blondie bites

Makes about **36**
Preparation time **15 minutes**
Cooking time **27 minutes**

40 g (1½ oz) **lightly salted
   butter**, plus extra for
   greasing
200 g (7 oz) **white chocolate**
2 **eggs**
65 g (2½ oz) **caster sugar**
1 teaspoon **vanilla bean
   paste**
75 g (3 oz) **self-raising flour**,
   sifted
50 g (2 oz) **blanched
   almonds**, roughly chopped

Grease and line a 20 cm (8 inch) square cake tin with
nonstick baking paper.

Chop half the chocolate into small pieces and set aside.
Roughly chop the remainder and put in a heatproof
bowl with the butter. Rest the bowl over a saucepan
of gently simmering water and leave until melted.

Beat together the eggs, sugar and vanilla bean paste in
a separate bowl. Beat in the melted chocolate mixture.
Add the flour, almonds and chopped chocolate and stir
well. Turn into the tin and spread into the corners.

Bake in a preheated oven, 190°C (375°F), Gas Mark
5, for about 25 minutes, or until the surface is golden
and the centre feels just firm to the touch. Leave to cool
completely before removing from the tin and cutting
into small squares.

For gluten-free chocolate brownies, grease and
line a 28 x 20 cm (11 x 8 inch) shallow baking tin
with nonstick baking paper. Chop 200 g (7 oz) milk
chocolate into small pieces. Melt 200 g (7 oz) plain
chocolate with 200 g (7 oz) unsalted butter, stirring
frequently until smooth. In a separate bowl, beat
together 3 eggs and 175 g (6 oz) light muscovado
sugar until turning foamy. Beat in the chocolate mixture.
Sift 75 g (3 oz) gluten-free flour and 2 teaspoons
gluten-free baking powder into the bowl. Add the
chopped chocolate and 100 g (3½ oz) walnut pieces.
Turn into the tin, level the surface and bake as above,
adding a little extra cooking time if the surface
feels very soft.

cherry bakewells

Makes about **30**
Preparation time **20 minutes**,
  plus chilling and cooling
Cooking time **1 hour**

350 g (11½ oz) **ready-made
dessert shortcrust pastry**
6 tablespoons **cherry
conserve**
125 g (4 oz) **lightly salted
butter**, softened
125 g (4 oz) **golden caster
sugar**
2 **eggs**
1 teaspoon **almond extract**
100 g (3½ oz) **ground
almonds**
125 g (4 oz) **self-raising flour**
½ teaspoon **baking powder**
200 g (7 oz) **natural glacé
cherries**, halved
40 g (1½ oz) **flaked almonds**

Glaze
50 g (2 oz) **icing sugar**, sifted
2 teaspoons **lemon juice**

Roll out the pastry thinly on a lightly floured surface and use to line the base and sides of a 28 x 18 cm (11 x 7 inch) shallow baking tin. Chill for 30 minutes.

Line the pastry case with nonstick baking paper and baking beans. Bake in a preheated oven, 200°C (400°F), Gas Mark 6, for 15 minutes. Remove the paper and beans and cook for a further 5 minutes. Reduce the oven temperature to 180°C (350°F), Gas Mark 4.

Spread the cherry conserve over the base of the pastry case. Put the butter, sugar, eggs, almond extract and ground almonds in bowl, sift in the flour and baking powder and beat with a hand-held electric whisk until smooth and creamy. Stir in the cherries.

Spoon the filling out into the pastry case, spreading it gently so you don't dislodge the conserve. Level with the back of a spoon and scatter with flaked almonds. Bake for 40 minutes until risen and just firm to the touch. Leave to cool in the tin.

Make the glaze by beating together the icing sugar and lemon juice. Remove the cake from the tin and drizzle with the glaze. Serve cut into small slices.

For homemade cherry conserve, put 500 g (1 lb) halved and stoned cherries in a large saucepan with the juice of 2 lemons and 2 tablespoons water. Cook gently for about 5 minutes until the cherries have softened. Add 500 g (1 lb) granulated sugar and heat gently until the sugar has dissolved. Cook gently, stirring occasionally, for about 40 minutes until the liquid has reduced and thickened. Transfer to jam jars and cover with lids. Leave to cool, then refrigerate for up to 3 months.

tropical ginger cake

Makes **20 squares**
Preparation time **30 minutes**,
  plus cooling
Cooking time **25 minutes**

150 g (5 oz) **butter**, plus extra
  for greasing
125 g (4 oz) **light muscovado
sugar**
3 tablespoons **golden syrup**
250 g (8 oz) **self-raising flour**
1 teaspoon **baking powder**
3 teaspoons **ground ginger**
50 g (2 oz) **desiccated
coconut**
3 **eggs**, beaten
200 g (7 oz) **canned
pineapple rings**, drained
and chopped

Lime frosting
100 g (3½ oz) **unsalted
butter**, softened
200 g (7 oz) **icing sugar**,
  sifted
grated rind and juice of **1 lime**

To decorate
ready-to-eat dried papaya
  and **apricot**, diced
few **dried coconut shavings**,
  for sprinkling

Grease and line the base of an 18 x 28 cm (7 x 11 inch) roasting tin with nonstick baking paper. Heat the butter, sugar and syrup gently in a saucepan, stirring until melted.

Mix the dry ingredients together in a mixing bowl, then stir in the melted butter mixture and beat together until smooth. Stir in the eggs, then the chopped pineapple. Turn into the tin and level the surface.

Bake in a preheated oven, 180°C (350°F), Gas Mark 4, for about 20 minutes until well risen and firm to touch. Leave to cool in the tin for 10 minutes then transfer to a wire rack.

Make the lime frosting by beating the butter, icing sugar and half the lime rind and juice together to make a smooth light mixture. Turn the cake over so the top is uppermost, then spread with the frosting. Decorate with a sprinkling of the remaining lime rind, ready-to-eat dried fruits and coconut shavings. Cut into 20 squares to serve.

For ginger muffin slice, grease and line a 750 g–1 kg (1½–2 lb) loaf tin with nonstick baking paper. Beat together 100 g (3½ oz) melted lightly salted butter, 175 ml (6 fl oz) milk and 1 egg. Mix together 250 g (8 oz) plain flour, 2 teaspoons baking powder, 2 teaspoons ground ginger, 150 g (5 oz) golden caster sugar, 25 g (1 oz) oatmeal and 75 g (3 oz) raisins in a bowl. Stir in the milk mixture until just combined and turn into the tin. Bake in a preheated oven, 180°C (350°F), Gas Mark 4 for about 45 minutes until risen and just firm. Dust with caster sugar and serve freshly baked.

sticky toffee & date squares

Makes **24** squares
Preparation time **25 minutes**,
  plus cooling
Cooking time **55 minutes**

200 g (7 oz) **lightly salted butter,** softened, plus extra for greasing
225 g (7½ oz) **stoned dates,** chopped
150 ml (¼ pint) **water**
150 ml (¼ pint) **double cream**
175 g (6 oz) **light muscovado sugar**
100 g (3½ oz) **caster sugar**
2 teaspoons **vanilla bean paste**
3 **eggs**
175 g (6 oz) **self-raising flour**
½ teaspoon **baking powder**

Grease and line a 28 x 18 cm (11 x 7 inch) shallow baking tin with nonstick baking paper. Put 125 g (4 oz) of the dates in a saucepan with the water and bring to the boil. Reduce the heat and cook gently for 5 minutes or until the dates are pulpy. Turn into a bowl and leave to cool. Put the cream, muscovado sugar and 75 g (3 oz) of the butter in a small saucepan and heat gently until the sugar dissolves. Bring to the boil and boil for 5 minutes or until thickened and caramelized. Leave to cool.

Put the remaining butter in a bowl with the caster sugar, vanilla bean paste and eggs, sift in the flour and baking powder and beat with a hand-held electric whisk until pale and creamy. Beat in the cooked dates and 100 ml (3½ fl oz) of the caramel mixture. Turn into the tin and level the surface. Scatter with the remaining dates.

Bake in a preheated oven, 180°C (350°F), Gas Mark 4, for 25 minutes, or until just firm. Spoon the remaining caramel on top and return to the oven for 15 minutes until the caramel has firmed. Transfer to a wire rack to cool.

For cider-glazed apple slice, grease the tin as above. Put 175 g (6 oz) lightly salted softened butter, 175 g (6 oz) golden caster sugar, 200 g (7 oz) sifted self-raising flour, ½ teaspoon baking powder, 1 teaspoon ground mixed spice and 3 eggs in a bowl and beat with a hand-held electric whisk until smooth and creamy. Stir in 65 g (2½ oz) sultanas and spread in the tin. Core and slice 2 small red apples and scatter over the surface. Bake as above for 40 minutes or until just firm. Put 100 ml (3½ fl oz) cider in a saucepan and heat until reduced to about 1 tablespoon. Cool and mix with 75 g (3 oz) sifted golden icing sugar until smooth. Drizzle over the cake.

coconut & rosewater slice

Makes **25 squares**
Preparation time **20 minutes**,
  plus cooling
Cooking time **40 minutes**

100 g (3½ oz) **almond** or
  coconut biscuits
40 g (1½ oz) **unsalted butter**,
  melted
400 ml (14 fl oz) **coconut milk**
150 ml (¼ pint) **double cream**
2 **eggs** plus 4 **egg yolks**
75 g (3 oz) **caster sugar**
15 g (½ oz) **plain flour**
1 teaspoon **rosewater**
50 g (2 oz) **rose Turkish
  delight**, chopped
pink food colouring (optional)

Dampen an 18 cm (7 inch) square, loose-based shallow tin or cake tin and line with a square of cling-film that comes up and over the sides. Crush the biscuits in a polythene bag with a rolling pin. Mix with the melted butter and tip into the tin, pressing down well.

Pour the coconut milk and cream into a saucepan and heat gently until bubbling around the edges. Put the eggs, egg yolks, sugar, flour and rosewater in a bowl and whisk until smooth. Pour the warmed milk over the egg mixture, whisking well. Strain through a sieve into a jug and spoon carefully over the biscuit base. Place a roasting tin of hot water on the lower oven shelf and place the tin on the upper shelf. Bake at 160°C (325°F), Gas Mark 3, for 35 minutes until the surface feels set but is still slightly wobbly. Leave to cool in the tin.

Put the Turkish delight in a small saucepan with 2 tablespoons water and heat gently to melt, stirring often. Add a little water if it evaporates. Add a drop of pink food colouring, drizzle the syrup over and cut into squares.

For coconut-frosted pineapple slice, beat 175 g (6 oz) softened unsalted butter, 175 g (6 oz) light muscovado sugar, 3 eggs, 200 g (7 oz) sifted self-raising flour and 1 teaspoon ground cinnamon in a bowl and spread into a greased and lined 28 x 18 cm (11 x 7 inch) shallow baking tin. Scatter with 150 g (5 oz) chopped glacé pineapple and bake at 180°C (350°F), Gas Mark 4, for about 40 minutes, or until just firm. Heat 5 tablespoons single cream and 50 g (2 oz) creamed coconut in a small pan until smooth. Whisk in 1 tablespoon lime juice and 300 g (10 oz) sifted icing sugar until smooth. Spread over the top.

buttery breton cake

Makes **25 squares**
Preparation time **25 minutes**,
   plus chilling and cooling
Cooking time **45 minutes**

225 g (7½ oz) **self-
   raising flour**, plus extra for
   dusting
175 g (6 oz) **icing sugar**
2 tablespoons **vanilla sugar**
   (see page 168) plus extra for
   dusting
200 g (7 oz) chilled **lightly
   salted butter**, diced, plus
   extra for greasing
5 **egg yolks**, plus 1 beaten
   egg, to glaze
150 g (5 oz) **strawberry jam**

Sift the flour and icing sugar into a food processor, add the vanilla sugar and butter and blend until the mixture resembles coarse breadcrumbs. Add the egg yolks and blend to make a thick paste. Wrap in clingfilm and chill for at least 3 hours or overnight.

Grease and line an 18–19 cm (7–7½ inch) square shallow baking tin with nonstick baking paper. Press half the dough into the tin, spreading it into the corners with your fingers so the dough forms an even layer. Spread the jam over the dough, leaving 1 cm (½ inch) clear around the edges.

Roll out the remaining dough on a floured surface to the same dimensions as the tin and lift into place. Press down gently and brush with the beaten egg. Bake in a preheated oven, 190°C (375°F), Gas Mark 5, for 40–45 minutes until risen and deep golden. Leave to cool in the tin before transferring to a flat plate or board. Dust lightly with vanilla sugar and cut into 25 squares.

For homemade strawberry jam, tip 1 kg (2 lb) strawberries into a large saucepan or preserving pan and add the juice of 4 lemons. Cook gently for 10 minutes or until the strawberries are soft. Add 1 kg (2 lb) granulated or preserving sugar and heat until the sugar dissolves. Boil for about 15–20 minutes until setting point is reached. To test for setting point, put a teaspoonful of the jam on a chilled saucer and place in the fridge for 2 minutes. Push the cooled jam with your finger. If the surface wrinkles, then setting point is reached. If still syrupy, boil the jam for a little longer. Avoid boiling the jam for too long or it will lose its strawberry flavour. Put into sterilized jars, cover and label.

passion cake squares

Makes **16**
Preparation time **10 minutes**,
    plus cooling
Cooking time **1 hour**

butter, for greasing
    175 g (6 oz) **brown rice
    flour**, plus extra for dusting
2 teaspoons **baking powder**
1 teaspoon **xanthan gum**
1 teaspoon **ground cinnamon**
375 g (12 oz) **caster sugar**
150 ml (¼ pint) **rapeseed** or
    corn oil
2 **eggs**, beaten
few drops of **vanilla extract**
375 g (12 oz) **carrots**, grated
50 g (2 oz) **desiccated
    coconut**
100 g (3½ oz) **canned
    crushed pineapple**, drained
50 g (2 oz) **sultanas**

Topping
200 g (7 oz) **cream cheese**
2 tablespoons **clear honey**
75 g (3 oz) **walnuts**, chopped
    (optional)

Grease a 20 cm (8 inch) square cake tin and dust with flour.

Sift together the flour, baking powder, xanthan gum and cinnamon in a large bowl. Add the sugar, oil, eggs and vanilla extract and beat well. Fold in the carrots, coconut, pineapple and sultanas. Turn into the tin and level the flour surface.

Bake in a preheated oven, 180°C (350°F), Gas Mark 4, for about 1 hour, or until a skewer inserted in the centre comes out clean. Leave to cool in the tin.

Beat together the cream cheese and honey and spread over the cake with a palette knife, then sprinkle the nuts on top, if using. Cut into 16 squares.

For mango & ginger cakes, make the cake mixture as above, using 2 teaspoons ground ginger instead of the cinnamon. Peel and stone 1 small ripe mango and chop into small pieces. Fold into the batter with the carrots, coconut and 50 g (2 oz) chopped Brazil nuts, omitting the pineapple and sultanas. Bake as above. Finely chop 50 g (2 oz) crystallized ginger. Mix 65 g (2½ oz) icing sugar with 1½–2 teaspoons water to make a glaze. Drizzle over the cake and scatter with the ginger.

stollen slice

Makes **15 slices**
Preparation time **30 minutes**,
 plus proving
Cooking time **25 minutes**

40 g (1½ oz) **salted butter**,
 plus extra for greasing
175 g (6 oz) **strong white
 bread flour**, plus extra for
 dusting
1½ teaspoons **fast-action
 dried yeast**
½ teaspoon **ground mixed
 spice**
25 g (1 oz) **caster sugar**
100 ml (3½ fl oz) warm **milk**
75 g (3 oz) **sultanas**
25 g (1 oz) chopped **almonds**
25 g (1 oz) chopped **candied
 peel**
150 g (5 oz) **marzipan**
icing sugar, for dusting

Grease a large loaf tin with a base measurement of about 25 x 10 cm (10 x 4 inches). Put the flour, yeast, mixed spice and sugar in a bowl. Melt 25 g (1 oz) of the butter, mix with the milk and add to the bowl. Mix with a round-bladed knife to make a soft but not sticky dough. Turn out onto a lightly floured surface and knead for 10 minutes until smooth and elastic. (Alternatively, use a freestanding mixer with a dough hook and knead for 5 minutes.) Place in a lightly oiled bowl, cover with clingfilm and leave to rise in a warm place for about 1½ hours or until doubled in size.

Turn the dough out onto a floured surface and knead in the sultanas, almonds and candied peel. Cover loosely with a tea towel and leave to rest for 10 minutes. Roll out the dough on a floured surface to a 25 x 20 cm (10 x 8 inch) rectangle. Roll the marzipan under the palms of your hands to form a log shape about 23 cm (9 inches) long and flatten to about 5 mm (¼ inch) thick. Lay the marzipan down the length of the dough, slightly to one side, and fold the rest of the dough over it. Transfer to the tin and press down gently.

Cover loosely with oiled clingfilm and leave to rise in a warm place for about 30 minutes until slightly risen. Remove the clingfilm. Bake in a preheated oven, 220°C (425°F), Gas Mark 7, for 25 minutes until risen and golden. Leave for 5 minutes, then turn out of the tin, place on a wire rack, cover with a sheet of foil and place a couple of food cans or pack of icing sugar on top to keep the stollen compact, while cooling on the wire rack. Melt the remaining butter and brush over the bread. Dust generously with icing sugar.

lemon drizzle bites

Makes **25**
Preparation time **15 minutes**
Cooking time **25 minutes**

125 g (4 oz) **lightly salted butter**, softened, plus extra for greasing
125 g (4 oz) **caster sugar**
finely grated rind and juice of 2 large **lemons**
2 **eggs**, beaten
125 g (4 oz) **self-raising flour**, sifted
65 g (2½ oz) **ground almonds**
75 g (3 oz) **granulated sugar**

Grease and line a 20 cm (8 inch) square, or similar-sized, loose-based tin with nonstick baking paper. Grease the paper.

Beat together the butter, caster sugar and lemon rind in a bowl until light and fluffy. Gradually beat in the eggs, adding a little flour to prevent the mixture curdling. Add the remaining flour and the ground almonds and fold the ingredients together gently until just combined. Turn into the tin and level the surface.

Bake in a preheated oven, 180°C (350°F), Gas Mark 4, for about 25 minutes until just firm to the touch. Transfer to a wire rack. While still warm, sprinkle the granulated sugar in a thick layer over the cake and drizzle with the lemon juice. Leave to cool completely. Cut into 25 small slices.

For almond-coffee cake, sprinkle 2 teaspoons espresso coffee powder into 2 tablespoons boiling water. Make the sponge mixture as above, omitting the lemon rind, and turn into the tin. Spoon the coffee mixture over the mixture so it is fairly evenly distributed. Use a knife to swirl the coffee mixture into the sponge to produce a rippled appearance. Toss 50 g (2 oz) flaked almonds with 1 tablespoon caster sugar and ½ teaspoon ground mixed spice and scatter over the surface. Bake as above.

pomegranate & ginger slice

Makes about **20 squares**
Preparation time **25 minutes**,
  plus cooling
Cooking time **50 minutes**

75 g (3 oz) **unsalted butter**,
  plus extra for greasing
200 g (7 oz) **plain flour**
1 teaspoon **bicarbonate of
  soda**
100 ml (3½ fl oz) **milk**
1 **egg**
100 g (3½ oz) **dark
  muscovado sugar**
125 g (4 oz) **black treacle**
3 pieces of **preserved stem
  ginger in syrup**, chopped

Topping
300 ml (½ pint) **pomegranate
  juice**
2 tablespoons **clear honey**
1 **pomegranate**

Grease and line 2 loaf tins, each with a base measurement of approximately 20 x 8 cm (8 x 3¼ inches), with nonstick baking paper.

Sift the flour and bicarbonate of soda into a bowl. Beat together the milk and egg. Put the sugar, treacle and butter in a saucepan and heat gently until the butter melts and the sugar dissolves. Remove from the heat and add to the milk mixture along with the chopped ginger. Add to the dry ingredients. Using a large, metal spoon, stir well until combined. Turn into the tins and level the surface.

Bake in a preheated oven, 160°C (325°F), Gas Mark 3, for 30 minutes, or until just firm to the touch and a skewer inserted in the centre comes out clean. Leave to cool in the tins, then transfer to a wire rack.

Pour the pomegranate juice into a saucepan and bring to the boil, then boil for about 15 minutes until thick and syrupy and reduced to about 3 tablespoons. Stir in the honey. Halve the pomegranate and push the halves inside out to release the fleshy seeds, discarding any white membrane, and scatter over the cakes. Drizzle with the syrup and cut into small squares to serve.

For sultana & lemon gingerbread, make the gingerbread mixture as above, reducing the milk by 25 ml (1 fl oz) and sprinkling 75 g (3 oz) sultanas over the mixture in the tin. After baking, leave to cool, then drizzle with lines of glacé icing made by mixing together 75 g (3 oz) sifted golden icing sugar with 2 teaspoons lemon juice.

cookies & cream fudge

Makes **36 pieces**
Preparation time **10 minutes**,
  plus cooling and chilling
Cooking time **15 minutes**

125 g (4 oz) **butter**, plus extra
  for greasing
200 ml (7 fl oz) **evaporated
  milk**
450 g (14½ oz) **golden
  caster sugar**
50 ml (2 fl oz) **water**
2 teaspoons **vanilla extract**
75 g (3 oz) **plain dark
  chocolate**, chopped
8 **Oreo cookies** or **bourbon
  biscuits**, chopped

Grease a 500 g (1 lb) loaf tin.

Heat the butter, evaporated milk, caster sugar, measurement water and vanilla extract gently together in a heavy-based pan, stirring until the sugar has dissolved. Bring to the boil and boil the mixture for 10 minutes, stirring all the time. Test to see if it is ready by carefully dropping ½ teaspoon of the mixture into some cold water – it should form a soft ball. Pour half the fudge mixture quickly into a heatproof jug. Add the chocolate to the remaining fudge mixture in the pan and stir to melt.

Pour half the chocolate fudge into the base of the loaf tin, then carefully scatter over half the biscuits. Pour the vanilla fudge on top and scatter over the remainder of the biscuits. Finish with a final layer of chocolate fudge. Cool, cover with clingfilm and chill overnight.

Turn out the fudge onto a board and cut into pieces.

For chocolate, orange & walnut fudge, prepare the fudge mixture as above, stirring in 75 g (3 oz) orange-flavoured dark chocolate in place of the plain dark chocolate. Replace the Oreo cookies or bourbon biscuits with 100 g (3½ oz) chopped walnuts. Finish as above.

sour cherry buns

Makes **16**

Preparation time **30 minutes**, plus proving

Cooking time **25 minutes**

250 g (8 oz) **strong white bread flour**, plus extra for dusting

2 teaspoons **fast-action dried yeast**

40 g (1½ oz) **caster sugar**

finely grated rind of 1 **lemon**

65 g (2½ oz) **salted butter, softened**, plus extra for greasing

1 **egg**

100 ml (3½ fl oz) warm **milk**

½ teaspoon **almond extract**

125 g (4 oz) **dried sour cherries**, chopped

25 g (1 oz) **light muscovado sugar**

Glaze

2 tablespoons **golden syrup**

2 tablespoons **lemon juice**

Put the flour, yeast, sugar and lemon rind in a bowl. Melt 40 g (1½ oz) of the butter. Beat the egg with the milk, melted butter and almond extract and add to the bowl. Mix with a round-bladed knife to make a soft but not sticky dough. Turn out onto a lightly floured surface and knead for 10 minutes until smooth and elastic.

Place in a lightly oiled bowl, cover with clingfilm and leave to rise in a warm place for 1½ hours or until doubled in size. Grease an 18 cm (7 inch) square cake tin, preferably loose based. Turn the dough onto a floured surface and roll out to a 50 x 15 cm (28 x 6 inch) rectangle. Spread with the soft butter and scatter with chopped sour cherries and muscovado sugar.

Roll up the dough from a long edge, so it forms a thin log, and cut across into 16 even-sized pieces. Lay the slices in the tin, cut sides up. Cover with oiled clingfilm and leave in a warm place for about 1 hour until the dough has risen. Bake in a preheated oven, 220°C (425°F), Gas Mark 7, for 25 minutes until risen and golden. Leave for 5 minutes then transfer to a rack to cool. Mix the syrup and lemon juice and use to glaze.

For cardamom & apricot buns, crush 12 cardamom pods until the shells split. Discard the shells and crush the seeds until coarsely ground. Make the dough as above, using orange rind instead of lemon, crushed cardamom instead of almond extract and plump dried apricots instead of cherries, and shape as before. For the icing mix 50 g (2 oz) sifted icing sugar with 1½ teaspoons orange juice and seeds of 5 crushed cardamom pods.

real chocolate brownies

Makes **10**
Preparation time **15 minutes**
Cooking time **25 minutes**

75 g (3 oz) **unsalted butter**,
  plus extra for greasing
75 g (3 oz) **plain dark
  chocolate**
2 **eggs**
250 g (8 oz) **golden caster
  sugar**
100 g (3½ oz) **plain flour**
½ teaspoon **baking powder**

Grease a 20 cm (8 inch) square tin and line the base
with nonstick baking paper.

Melt the butter and chocolate together in a saucepan
over a low heat. Whisk the eggs and sugar together
in a bowl until the mixture is pale and creamy. Stir the
melted chocolate mixture into the egg mixture. Sift in
the flour and baking powder and fold together. Turn into
the tin and level the surface.

Bake in a preheated oven, 190°C (375°F), Gas Mark 5,
for 25 minutes until the brownies are firm on top and a
skewer inserted into the centre comes out clean. Cool
in the tin for 5 minutes, then cut into squares.

For rich chocolate mocha brownies, roughly
chop 100 g (3½ oz) pecan nuts. Dissolve 2 teaspoons
espresso coffee powder in 1 tablespoon hot water.
Chop 100 g (3½ oz) milk chocolate into small pieces.
Make the brownies as above, adding the coffee to
the melted chocolate and butter. Turn into the tin and
scatter with the chopped chocolate and nuts before
baking as above.

pastries

soft fruit tartlets

Makes **10–12**
Preparation time **30 minutes**,
  plus chilling and cooling
Cooking time **30 minutes**

100 g (3½ oz) **plain flour**,
  sifted
65 g (2½ oz) chilled **unsalted
  butter**, diced
50 g (2 oz) **icing sugar**,
  sifted, plus extra for dusting
  (optional)
3 **egg yolks**
3 teaspoons cold **water**
250 ml (8 fl oz) **double cream**
1 teaspoon **vanilla bean
  paste**
40 g (1½ oz) **caster sugar**
300 g (10 oz) small
  **strawberries, raspberries
  and redcurrants**
4 tablespoons **redcurrant jelly**

Put the flour and butter in a food processor and blend until the mixture resembles breadcrumbs. Add the icing sugar and blend briefly to mix. Add 1 of the egg yolks and 1 teaspoon of the measurement water and mix to a soft dough. Wrap in clingfilm and chill for at least 1 hour.

Use the dough to line 10–12 sections of a mini muffin or tartlet tin, each with a 50ml (2fl oz) capacity. Take 20 g (¾ oz) balls of the dough and push into the base of each section. Press the dough up the sides of sections, trim off the excess at the tops and chill for 30 minutes.

Line the cases with nonstick baking paper and fill with baking beans. Bake in a preheated oven, 200°C (400°F), Gas Mark 6, for 15 minutes. Remove from the oven and lift out the beans and paper. Reduce the oven temperature to 160°C (325°F), Gas Mark 3.

Beat together the cream, remaining egg yolks, vanilla bean paste and caster sugar and pour into the cases. Bake for about 15 minutes until the filling is lightly set. Leave to cool in the tins, remove and pile the fruits on top of the pastries. Melt the redcurrant jelly in a small saucepan with the remaining water until smooth and syrupy and use to glaze the tartlets.

For maple & walnut tartlets, make the dough as above, adding ½ teaspoon ground mixed spice. Press into the tin sections, making a dip in the centre of each rather than pressing it right up the sides. Chop 75 g (3 oz) pecan nuts and push into the pastries. Drizzle each with ½ teaspoon maple syrup and bake at 180°C (350°F), Gas Mark 4, for 20 minutes until golden. Transfer to a rack to cool, drizzle with a little maple syrup and serve.

almond praline buns

Makes **16**

Preparation time **30 minutes**, plus cooling

Cooking time **30 minutes**

50g (2 oz) chilled **unsalted butter**, diced

5 tablespoons **milk**

5 tablespoons **water**

75g (3 oz) **plain flour**, sifted

2 **eggs**, beaten

40 g (1½ oz) **flaked almonds**

2 tablespoons **caster sugar**

150 ml (¼ pint) **double cream**

2 tablespoons **almond liqueur**

icing sugar, for dusting

Place 16 mini silicone muffin cases on a baking sheet. Put the butter in a small saucepan with the milk and water. Heat gently until the butter dissolves. Bring to the boil and remove from the heat. Tip in the flour and beat well until the mixture forms a smooth ball that leaves the sides of the pan. Leave to cool for 2 minutes. Gradually beat the eggs into the paste, until it is smooth and glossy. Push a teaspoonful of the choux pastry into a case. Fill the remainder in the same way. Lightly crumble 15 g (½ oz) of the almonds and scatter over the pastry.

Bake in a preheated oven, 200°C (400°F), Gas Mark 6, for about 20 minutes until risen and golden. Remove from the oven, take out of the cases and make a small horizontal slit in the side of each bun. Return to the oven for a further 3 minutes. Transfer to a wire rack to cool. Scatter the remaining almonds onto a baking sheet lined with nonstick baking paper and sprinkle the caster sugar on top. Place under a moderate grill for about 5 minutes until the sugar starts to caramelize. Leave to cool. Turn the mixture into a food processor and blend until finely ground. Whip the cream with the liqueur until it holds its shape. Stir in the ground praline, spoon into pastries. Dust with icing sugar.

For crème pâtissière buns, make the buns as above. Put 150 ml (¼ pint) single cream in a saucepan with 1 teaspoon vanilla extract and bring to the boil. Beat together 2 egg yolks, 20 g (¾ oz) caster sugar and 1 tablespoon plain flour in a bowl. Beat in the hot milk. Return to the saucepan and cook over a gentle heat, stirring constantly until thickened. Turn into a small bowl, cover with greaseproof paper and cool. Use to fill the buns.

pineapple & rum puffs

Makes **25**
Preparation time **30 minutes**,
   plus cooling
Cooking time **20 minutes**

½ juicy ripe **pineapple**
50 g (2 oz) **raisins**
3 tablespoons **clear honey**
4 tablespoons **rum**
butter, for greasing
500 g (1 lb) **ready-made
   puff pastry**
flour, for dusting
1 **egg yolk**
200 g (7 oz) **mascarpone
   cheese**
2 tablespoons **icing sugar**,
   sifted

Cut away the skin from the pineapple and cut the flesh into thin slices. Chop the pineapple into small pieces, discarding the central core. Put in a bowl and stir in the raisins, 2 tablespoons of the honey and 2 tablespoons of the rum.

Grease a baking sheet. Roll out the pastry on a lightly floured surface to a 28 cm (11 inch) square. Trim off the edges and cut into 5 even-sized strips. Cut across in the opposite direction to make 25 squares. Using the tip of a sharp knife, make a shallow cut, 1 cm (½ inch) away from the edges, to make a rim. Beat the egg yolk with the remaining honey and brush over the pastry rims.

Bake in a preheated oven, 220°C (425°F), Gas Mark 7, for 15 minutes, or until risen and golden. Scoop out the centres of the pastries to shape cases and return to the oven for 5 minutes. Transfer to a wire rack to cool. Beat the mascarpone with the icing sugar and remaining rum and spoon into the cases. Pile the pineapple mixture on top to serve.

For rhubarb & orange puffs, cut 300 g (10 oz) young rhubarb into 1 cm (½ inch) pieces and put in a saucepan with 100 g (3½ oz) caster sugar and the finely grated rind and juice of 1 orange. Cook gently until the rhubarb is just tender. Drain the rhubarb into a bowl. Mix 1 teaspoon cornflour with 1 tablespoon water and add to the juices in the pan. Cook, stirring until thickened. Add to the rhubarb and leave to cool. Make and cook the pastry cases as above. Beat 2 tablespoons sifted icing sugar into 200 g (7 oz) cream cheese and spoon into the cases. Pile the rhubarb on top to serve.

chocolate eclairs & cream liqueur

Makes **18**
Preparation time **40 minutes**,
  plus cooling
Cooking time **15 minutes**

50 g (2 oz) **unsalted butter**,
  plus extra for greasing
150 ml (¼ pint) **water**
65 g (2½ oz) **plain flour**, sifted
2 **eggs**, beaten
½ teaspoon **vanilla extract**

Filling
250 ml (8 fl oz) **double cream**
2 tablespoons **icing sugar**
4 tablespoons **whisky** and
  coffee cream liqueur

Topping
25 g (1 oz) **unsalted butter**
100 g (3½ oz) **plain dark
  chocolate**, broken into
  pieces
1 tablespoon **icing sugar**
2–3 teaspoons **milk**

Grease a large baking sheet.

Heat the butter and measurement water gently in a saucepan until melted. Bring to the boil, then add the flour all at once and beat the mixture until it forms a smooth ball that leaves the sides of the pan almost clean. Leave to cool for 2 minutes.

Beat the eggs and vanilla extract into the paste gradually until thick and smooth. Spoon the choux pastry into a large piping bag fitted with a 1 cm (½ inch) plain nozzle, and pipe 7 cm (3 inch) lines of pastry onto the baking sheet.

Bake in a preheated oven, 200°C (400°F), Gas Mark 6, for 15 minutes until well risen. Make a slit in the side of each éclair for the steam to escape, then return to the turned-off oven for 5 minutes. Leave to cool.

Whip the cream for the filling to soft swirls, then gradually whisk in the icing sugar and liqueur. Slit each éclair lengthways and spoon or pipe in the cream. Make the chocolate topping by heating the butter, chocolate and icing sugar together gently until just melted. Stir in the milk, then spoon over the top of the éclairs. These are best eaten on the day they are made.

For citrus iced buns, make and bake the éclairs as above. Make the filling, replacing the whisky or coffee liqueur with an orange-flavoured liqueur or freshly squeezed orange juice. Use to fill the buns. Put 200 g (7 oz) fondant icing sugar in a bowl and stir in enough lemon juice to make an icing that thickly coats the back of the spoon. Add a drop of natural yellow food colouring, if liked. Spoon over the top of the éclairs.

plum tripiti

Makes **24**
Preparation time **40 minutes**
Cooking time **10 minutes**

75 g (3 oz) **unsalted butter**,
   melted
100 g (3½ oz) **feta cheese**,
   drained and coarsely grated
100 g (3 oz) **ricotta cheese**
50 g (2 oz) **caster sugar**
¼ teaspoon **ground
   cinnamon**
1 **egg**, beaten
12 sheets of **filo pastry**
flour, for dusting
500 g (1 lb) small **red plums**,
   halved and pitted
icing sugar, for dusting

Grease a baking sheet with some of the melted butter.
Mix the feta, ricotta, sugar, cinnamon and egg in a bowl.

Unfold the pastry sheets on a lightly floured surface,
then put one in front of you, with a short side facing you
(covering the others with clingfilm). Brush the pastry
sheet with a little of the melted butter, then cut in half
to make 2 long strips.

Place a spoonful of the cheese mixture a little up from
the bottom left-hand corner of each strip, then cover
with a plum half. Fold the bottom right-hand corner of
one strip diagonally over the plum to cover the filling
and to make a triangle. Fold the bottom left-hand corner
upwards to make a second triangle, then keep folding
until the top of the strip is reached and the filling is
enclosed. Place on the baking sheet and repeat until 24
triangles have been made using all the filling. Brush the
outside of the triangles with the remaining butter.

Bake in a preheated oven, 200°C (400°F), Gas Mark
6, for about 10 minutes until the pastry is golden and
the plum juices begin to run from the sides. Dust with a
little sifted icing sugar and leave to cool for 15 minutes
before serving.

For pear & cream cheese triangles, make the filling
as above, using 100 g (3½ oz) cream cheese to replace
the feta and adding 1 teaspoon vanilla bean paste with
the cinnamon. Peel, core and dice 3 ripe juicy pears and
toss with 2 teaspoons lemon juice to prevent them from
browning. Assemble the pastries, spooning the diced
pears onto the cream cheese mixture. After baking,
dust with caster sugar and serve warm or cold.

tangy lemon squares

Makes **16**
Preparation time **25 minutes**,
  plus chilling and cooling
Cooking time **45 minutes**

100 g (3½ oz) **plain flour**,
  sifted, plus extra for dusting
175 g (6 oz) chilled **unsalted
  butter**, cut into pieces
40 g (1½ oz) **icing sugar**,
  sifted, plus extra for dusting
1 teaspoon cold **water**
1 **egg yolk** and 6 **eggs**,
  beaten
300 g (10 oz) **caster sugar**
finely grated rind and juice of
  4 **lemons**

Put the flour and 50 g (2 oz) of the butter in a food processor and blend until the mixture resembles breadcrumbs. Add the icing sugar, measurement water and egg yolk and blend to make a soft dough. Wrap in clingfilm and chill for at least 30 minutes.

Roll out the dough thinly on a floured surface to a 21 cm (8½ inch) square. Fit into a 20 cm (8 inch) square loose-based cake tin or shallow baking tin, pressing the pastry down firmly around the edges. Bake in a preheated oven, 200°C (400°F), Gas Mark 6, for 15 minutes. Remove from the oven and reduce the oven temperature to 180°C (350°F), Gas Mark 4. Put the whole eggs, caster sugar and remaining butter into a saucepan and heat gently until the sugar has dissolved. Stir in the lemon rind and juice and cook, stirring, for 5–10 minutes until the mixture has thickened slightly. Strain through a sieve into a jug and pour over the pastry.

Bake for 20 minutes until just set. Leave to cool completely in the tin. Transfer to a plate, dust with icing sugar and serve cut into 16 squares.

For meringue-frosted lime squares, prepare and bake the pastry as above. Make the filling, replacing 3 of the lemons and the lemon rind with the rind and juice of 4 limes. Bake and leave to cool. Put 2 egg whites, 100 g (3½ oz) sifted icing sugar and a pinch of cream of tartar into a thoroughly clean heatproof bowl and rest it over a pan of gently simmering water. Whisk with a hand-held electric whisk until thickened. Remove from the heat and whisk for a further 2–3 minutes until softly peaking. Use a palette knife to spread the frosting over the filling.

honey, grape & cinnamon tartlets

Makes **16**
Preparation time **25 minutes**, plus cooling
Cooking time **10 minutes**

100 g (3½ oz) **seedless red grapes**, peeled and halved
100 g (3½ oz) **seedless white grapes**, peeled and halved
3 tablespoons **dessert wine** or **grape juice**
25 g (1 oz) **unsalted butter**, melted
½ teaspoon **ground cinnamon**
3 sheets of **filo pastry**
flour, for dusting
100 ml (3½ fl oz) **double cream**
100 ml (3½ fl oz) **Greek yogurt**
2 tablespoons **clear honey**, plus extra to drizzle

Place 16 mini silicone muffin cases on a baking sheet.

Put the grapes in a bowl with the wine or grape juice. Mix the melted butter with the cinnamon.

Unfold the pastry sheets on a lightly floured surface, then put one in front of you (covering the others with clingfilm). Cut into 6.5 cm (2¾ inch) squares. Brush the squares lightly with the spiced butter. Cut out more squares from the other 2 sheets and position over the first, adjusting the positions so the points are evenly staggered. Press into the cases and brush with a little more butter.

Bake in a preheated oven, 190°C (375°F), Gas Mark 5, for 10 minutes until golden. Transfer to a wire rack to cool.

Beat the cream with the yogurt and honey until just holding its shape. Drain the grapes over the cream so you can beat the juice into the cream. Spoon the cream mixture into the pastry cases and pile the grapes on top. Serve drizzled with extra honey.

For blueberry & cream cheese tartlets, make the filo cases as above, omitting the cinnamon from the butter. Beat 250 g (8 oz) cream cheese in a bowl with 1 teaspoon vanilla bean paste and 2 tablespoons sifted icing sugar until smooth. Spoon into the cases and top with blueberry conserve. Serve lightly dusted with icing sugar.

churros

Makes **12**

Preparation time **20 minutes**, plus cooling

Cooking time **10 minutes**

200 g (7 oz) **plain flour**
¼ teaspoon **salt**
5 tablespoons **caster sugar**
275 ml (9 fl oz) **water**
1 **egg**, beaten, plus 1 **egg yolk**
1 teaspoon **vanilla extract**
1 litre (1¾ pints) **sunflower oil**
1 teaspoon **ground cinnamon**

Mix the flour, salt and 1 tablespoon of the sugar in a bowl. Pour the water into a saucepan and bring to the boil. Take off the heat, add the flour mixture and beat well. Return to the heat and stir until it forms a smooth ball that leaves the sides of the pan almost clean. Remove from the heat and leave to cool for 10 minutes. Gradually beat the whole egg, egg yolk and vanilla extract into the flour mixture until smooth. Spoon into a large piping bag fitted with a 1 cm (½ inch) plain nozzle.

Pour the oil into a medium-sized saucepan to a depth of 2.5 cm (1 inch). Heat to 170°C (340°F) on a sugar thermometer. Alternatively, to test if the oil is hot enough, pipe a tiny amount of the mixture into the oil: if the oil bubbles instantly, it is ready to use. Pipe coils, S-shapes and squiggly lines into the oil, in small batches, cutting the ends off at the nozzle with kitchen scissors. Cook the churros for 2–3 minutes until they float and are golden, turning, if needed, to brown evenly.

Lift the churros out of the oil, drain well on kitchen paper, then sprinkle with the remaining sugar mixed with the cinnamon. Continue piping and frying until all the mixture has been used (probably 3 batches). Serve warm or cold. Best eaten on the day they are made.

For white chocolate sauce, put 1 tablespoon caster sugar in a small saucepan with ½ teaspoon ground ginger and 5 tablespoons water and heat gently until the sugar dissolves. Bring to the boil and remove from the heat. Add 150 g (5 oz) chopped white chocolate and leave until melted, stirring frequently until smooth. Stir in 5 tablespoons double cream. Serve with the churros for dipping.

citrus baklava

Makes **24**
Preparation time **30 minutes**,
   plus cooling and chilling
Cooking time **35 minutes**

400 g (13 oz) packet **filo
   pastry**
flour, for dusting
125 g (4 oz) **unsalted butter**,
   melted

Filling
100 g (3½ oz) **walnut pieces**
100 g (3½ oz) **shelled
   pistachio nuts**, plus extra
   slivers to decorate
100 g (3½ oz) **blanched
   almonds**
75 g (3 oz) **caster sugar**
½ teaspoon **ground
   cinnamon**

Syrup
1 **lemon**
1 small **orange**
250 g (8 oz) **caster sugar**
pinch of **ground cinnamon**
150 ml (¼ pint) **water**

Make the filling by dry-frying the nuts in a nonstick pan for 3–4 minutes, stirring until light brown. Leave to cool, then chop roughly and mix with sugar and cinnamon.

Unfold the pastry on a lightly floured surface and cut it into rectangles the same size as the base of an 18 x 28 cm (7 x 11 inch) small roasting tin. Wrap half the pastry in clingfilm so that it doesn't dry out. Brush each sheet of pastry with melted butter, then layer up in the roasting tin. Spoon in the nut mixture, unwrap and cover with the remaining pastry, buttering each layer. Cut the pastry into 6 squares, then cut each into 4 triangles.

Bake in a preheated oven, 180°C (350°F), Gas Mark 4, for 30–35 minutes, covering with foil after 20 minutes to prevent it overbrowning. Meanwhile, make the syrup. Pare the rind off the citrus fruits with a zester, then cut the rind into strips. Squeeze the juice. Put the strips and juice in a saucepan with the sugar, cinnamon and measurement water. Heat gently until the sugar dissolves, then simmer for 5 minutes without stirring.

Pour the hot syrup over the pastry as soon as it comes out of the oven. Leave to cool, then chill for 3 hours. Remove from the tin and arrange the pieces on a serving plate, sprinkled with slivers of pistachio. Store in the refrigerator for up to 2 days.

For baklava with spices, bake the baklava as above. Make the syrup, adding 1 teaspoon coriander seeds crushed with a pestle and mortar, ¼ teaspoon ground cloves and 1 teaspoon rosewater or orange flower water with the citrus fruit juice. Pour over the cooked baklava and finish as above.

blackberry & apple vol au vents

Makes **20**
Preparation time **15 minutes**
Cooking time about
  15 minutes

75 g (3 oz) **unsalted butter**
75 g (3 oz) **caster sugar**
2 small, crisp **dessert apples**
200 g (7 oz) small
  blackberries
1 teaspoon **vanilla bean
  paste**
2 teaspoons **lemon juice**
20 **vol au vent cases**

Melt the butter in a frying pan and stir in the sugar.
Cook over a gentle heat until the sugar dissolves.
Continue to cook until the mixture starts to caramelize.
Remove from the heat.

Peel, core and chop the apples into the pan and cook
gently for 3–5 minutes until the apples start to soften.
Add the blackberries and cook for a further minute.
Stir in the vanilla bean paste and lemon juice. Spoon
into the vol au vent cases, packing the mixture down
gently. Place on a baking sheet and cook in a preheated
oven, 180°C (350°F), Gas Mark 4, for 5 minutes to
warm through.

Reduce the syrup left in the frying pan for about 5
minutes until thickened, then spoon onto the fruits.
Lightly dust with icing sugar and serve decorated with
mint sprigs or edible flowers.

For homemade vol au vent cases, roll out 500 g
(1 lb) puff pastry to a generous 5 mm (¼ inch) thick.
Cut out circles using a 5 cm (2 inch) round cutter and
space slightly apart on a greased baking sheet. Layer
up the trimmings and reroll to cut more circles. Using
a 4 cm (1¾ inch) round cutter, impress circles in the
centres of the pastries, but don't press right through
to the baking sheet. Lift away the cutter. Brush the top
edges of the cases only with egg yolk to glaze and bake
in a preheated oven, 220°C (425°F), Gas Mark 7, for 12
minutes until golden and well risen. Remove from the
oven and lift out the risen pastry in the centres to leave
shells. Return to the oven for a further 5 minutes. Once
completely cool, store in an airtight container for up
to 2 days.

ginger profiteroles

Serves **4**

Preparation time **35 minutes**, plus cooling

Cooking time **20 minutes**

50 g (2 oz) **unsalted butter**, plus extra for greasing

150 ml (¼ pint) **water**

pinch of **salt**

65 g (2½ oz) **plain flour**, sifted

2 **eggs**

½ teaspoon **vanilla extract**

250 ml (8 fl oz) **double cream**

50 g (2 oz) **crystallized** or **glacé ginger**, finely chopped

Sauce

150 g (5 oz) **plain dark chocolate**, broken into pieces

150 ml (¼ pint) **milk**

50 g (2 oz) **caster sugar**

2 tablespoons **brandy**

Grease a large baking sheet. Pour the measurement water into a medium saucepan, add the butter and salt and heat until the butter has melted. Bring to the boil, then take off the heat and stir in the flour. Put the pan back on the heat and cook briefly, stirring until the mixture makes a smooth ball. Leave to cool.

Beat the eggs and vanilla extract into the paste gradually until smooth. Spoon the choux pastry into a large piping bag fitted with a 1.5 cm (¾ inch) plain nozzle, and pipe 20 balls onto the baking sheet, leaving space in between.

Bake in a preheated oven, 200°C (400°F), Gas Mark 6, for 15 minutes until well risen. Make a slit in the side of each ball for the steam to escape, then return to the turned-off oven for 5 minutes. Leave to cool.

Make the sauce by heating the chocolate, milk and sugar in a saucepan and stirring until smooth. Take off the heat and mix in the brandy. Whip the cream until it forms soft peaks, then fold in the ginger. Enlarge the slit in each profiterole and spoon in the ginger cream. Pile into serving dishes and drizzle with the reheated sauce.

For feathered chocolate profiteroles, make and bake the profiteroles as above. Whip 250 ml (8 fl oz) double cream with 1 tablespoon icing sugar and use to fill the profiteroles. Melt 150 g (5 oz) plain chocolate and 50 g (2 oz) white chocolate in separate bowls (see page 14). Spoon a little plain chocolate over the top of a bun and drizzle a little white chocolate over the top. Swirl the two chocolates together with the tip of a skewer to feather. Repeat with the remainder.

orange puffs

Makes **25**
Preparation time **25 minutes**
Cooking time **12 minutes**

butter, for greasing
250 g (8 oz) **ready-made puff pastry**
flour, for dusting
2 tablespoons **caster sugar**
finely grated rind of 1 **orange**
1 **egg yolk**

Buttercream
50 g (2 oz) **unsalted butter**, softened
75 g (3 oz) **icing sugar**, sifted, plus extra for dusting (optional)
1 tablespoon **orange juice**
1 tablespoon **lemon juice**

Grease a baking sheet. Roll out the pastry on a lightly floured surface to a 23 cm (9 inch) square and cut in half. Mix 1 tablespoon of the caster sugar with the orange rind and sprinkle over one half of the pastry. Lay the other half on top and re-roll the pastry to a 25 cm (10 inch) square. Trim off the edges to neaten.

Cut the pastry into 5 strips, then across in the opposite direction to make 25 squares. Transfer to the baking sheet, spacing them slightly apart, and prick all over with a fork. Bake in a preheated oven, 200°C (400°F), Gas Mark 6, for 10 minutes until risen and pale golden. Beat the egg yolk with the remaining caster sugar. Brush over the pastries and return to the oven for a further 2 minutes or until golden. Transfer to a wire rack to cool.

Make the buttercream by beating together the butter, icing sugar and orange and lemon juice. Split each pastry in half and sandwich with the buttercream. Dust lightly with icing sugar, if liked.

For cinnamon fruit puffs, thinly roll out 300 g (10 oz) puff pastry on a lightly floured surface and cut in half. Mix 2 tablespoons caster sugar with 1 teaspoon ground cinnamon and sprinkle over one half. Scatter with 75 g (3 oz) currants. Lay the second sheet of pastry on top of the first and re-roll until thin enough for the raisins to show through clearly. Transfer to a greased baking sheet and cut into rectangles measuring about 7 x 4 cm (3 x 1¾ inches). Brush with beaten egg and dust with caster sugar. Bake in a preheated oven, 200°C (400°F), Gas Mark 6, for about 15 minutes until golden. Transfer to a wire rack to cool.

chocolate filo twiglets

Makes **22**
Preparation time **20 minutes**
Cooking time **10 minutes**

50 g (2 oz) **unsalted butter**,
  melted, plus extra for
  greasing
100 g (3½ oz) **plain dark** or
  milk chocolate, chopped
25 g (1 oz) **hazelnuts**, toasted
  and chopped
25 g (1 oz) **raisins**, chopped
4 sheets of **filo pastry**
flour, for dusting
50 g (2 oz) **caster sugar**
½ teaspoon **ground
  cinnamon**

Grease a baking sheet.

Mix together the chocolate, hazelnuts and raisins.

Unfold the pastry sheets on a lightly floured surface, then put one in front of you (covering the others with clingfilm) and brush with a little of the melted butter. Place a second sheet on top. Cut the pastry into 12 x 6 cm (5 x 2½ inch) rectangles.

Sprinkle a heaped teaspoonful of the chocolate mixture in a line down the long edge of one strip, leaving a 1 cm (½ inch) area uncovered at either end. Fold the ends over the chocolate, then roll up, starting from the chocolate-covered side. Shape the remainder in the same way using the other sheets of filo, so that you have 22 in all. Brush the pastries with more butter.

Bake in a preheated oven, 220°C (425°F), Gas Mark 7, for about 10 minutes until deep golden.

Mix the sugar with the cinnamon and place on a plate. Roll the warm pastries in the spiced sugar until coated. Serve warm or transfer to a wire rack to cool.

For date & fresh ginger sticks, finely chop 200 g (7 oz) dates and mix in a bowl with 25 g (1 oz) finely chopped fresh ginger and 1 tablespoon clear honey. Use this mixture to fill the filo pastries, then bake as above. After baking, roll the pastries in the spiced sugar, using ground ginger instead of the cinnamon.

mini nectarine & blueberry tarts

Makes **12**
Preparation time **15 minutes**
Cooking time **8 minutes**

25 g (1 oz) **unsalted butter**
2 teaspoons **olive oil**
4 sheets of **filo pastry**
flour, for dusting
2 tablespoons **red berry jam**
juice of ½ **orange**
4 ripe **nectarines**, halved,
  pitted and sliced
150 g (5 oz) **blueberries**
icing sugar, for dusting

Heat the butter and oil in a small saucepan until the butter has melted.

Unfold the pastry on a lightly floured surface and separate into sheets. Brush lightly with the butter mixture, then cut into 24 pieces, each 10 x 8 cm (4 x 3½ inches).

Arrange a piece in each of the sections of a deep 12-hole muffin tin, then add a second piece at a slight angle to the first pieces to give a pretty jagged edge to each pastry case.

Bake in a preheated oven, 180°C (350°F), Gas Mark 4, for 6–8 minutes until golden. Meanwhile, warm the jam and orange juice in a saucepan, then add the nectarines and blueberries and warm through.

Lift the tart cases carefully out of the muffin tin and transfer to a serving dish. Fill the cases with the warm fruits and dust with sifted icing sugar. Serve with cream or ice cream (see below).

For mascarpone & vanilla ice cream, put 225 g (7½ oz) caster sugar in a saucepan with 450 ml (¾ pint) water and heat gently until the sugar dissolves. Bring to the boil and boil for 3 minutes. Remove from the heat, stir in 2 tablespoons lemon juice and leave to cool. Beat 500 g (1 lb) mascarpone cheese in a bowl with 2 teaspoons vanilla bean paste. Gradually beat in the cooled syrup. Churn in an ice cream machine and transfer to a freezer container. Freeze until ready to use. Serve scooped over the tarts.

spicy raisin palmiers

Makes **22**
Preparation time **15 minutes**,
  plus freezing
Cooking time **12 minutes**

butter, for greasing
75 g (3 oz) **raisins**, chopped
1 teaspoon **ground mixed
  spice**
2 tablespoons **caster sugar**
250 g (8 oz) **ready-made puff
  pastry**
flour, for dusting
1 **egg yolk**
1 teaspoon **water**

To serve
vanilla ice cream
Pedro Ximenez sherry, or any
  other **sweet, well-flavoured
  sherry**

Grease 2 baking sheets.

Mix together the raisins, spice and sugar. Roll out the pastry on a lightly floured surface to a 30 x 20 cm (12 x 8 inch) rectangle. Mix the egg yolk with the measurement water and brush some of it sparingly over the pastry, taking it right to the edges. Sprinkle with the raisin mixture. Roll up the pastry, starting from a long side, to shape a neat log. Wrap in clingfilm and freeze for 30 minutes.

Trim off the ends from the pastry log. Using a sharp knife, cut across into 22 slices, 1 cm (½ inch) wide. Roll lightly with a floured rolling pin to flatten slightly, then transfer to the baking sheets. Brush with the remaining egg yolk.

Bake in a preheated oven, 220°C (425°F), Gas Mark 7, for about 12 minutes until risen and golden. Serve warm or, if preferred, transfer to a wire rack and leave to cool a little or completely.

Drizzle with a little sherry to serve.

For mocha cream palmiers, blend 2 teaspoons espresso coffee powder with 2 teaspoons cocoa powder and 2 tablespoons vanilla sugar (see page 168). Make the pastries as above, using the coffee mixture instead of the raisin one. Bake as above. Melt 100 g (3½ oz) plain dark chocolate (see page 14), and stir in 4 tablespoons double cream. Once the chocolate cream is cold but not set, use it to sandwich the pastries together.

papaya, lime & mango tartlets

Makes **20**
Preparation time **35 minutes**, plus chilling
Cooking time **20 minutes**

250 g (8 oz) **chilled ready-made sweet shortcrust pastry**
flour, for dusting
thinly grated rind and juice of 2 large, juicy **limes**
6 tablespoons **double cream**
150 ml (¼ pint) **full-fat condensed milk**
2 tablespoons finely diced **mango**
2 tablespoons finely diced **papaya**
lime rind, to decorate

Roll out the pastry on a lightly floured surface to 2.5 mm (⅛ inch) thick and cut out 20 rounds using a 5 cm (2 inch) round cutter.

Use the pastry rounds to line 20 sections of 2 x 12-hole mini tartlet tins. Prick the pastry bases with a fork. Line with nonstick baking paper and fill with baking beans.

Bake in a preheated oven, 190°C (375°F), Gas Mark 5, for 10 minutes. Remove the paper and beans and return the cases to the oven for 5–10 minutes, or until they are crisp and golden. Leave to cool in the tins.

Put the lime rind in a blender with the cream and condensed milk and pulse until well combined. With the motor running, slowly pour in the lime juice and process until blended. (Alternatively, mix well by hand.) Transfer to a bowl, cover and chill in the refrigerator for 3–4 hours or until firm.

Put the pastry cases on a serving platter and spoon the lime mixture into each case. Mix the mango with the papaya and, using a teaspoon, top the cases with the fruit mixture. Decorate with lime rind and serve at once.

For raspberry cream tartlets, make the pastry cases and filling as above. Spoon the filling into the cases. Warm 4 tablespoons raspberry jam in a saucepan with the grated rind and juice of 1 lime. Cook for 1 minute until syrupy, then press through a sieve into a small bowl. Pile 300 g (10 oz) fresh raspberries onto the tartlets and drizzle with the syrup. Dust lightly with icing sugar.

meringues &
macaroons

brown sugar meringues

Makes **24**

Preparation time **25 minutes**, plus cooling

Cooking time **45 minutes**

butter, for greasing

65 g (2½ oz) **light muscovado sugar**

50 g (2 oz) **caster sugar**

2 **egg whites**

250 g (9 oz) **mascarpone cheese**

2 tablespoons **icing sugar**, sifted

2 tablespoons **milk**

1 teaspoon **vanilla bean paste**

Grease and line 2 baking sheets with nonstick baking paper. Mix the 2 sugars together.

Whisk the egg whites in a thoroughly clean bowl until stiffly peaking. Gradually whisk in the sugars, a dessertspoonful at a time and whisking well between each addition, until the mixture is stiff and glossy.

Spoon into a large piping bag fitted with a 1 cm (½ inch) star nozzle. Pipe 24 fingers, 6 cm (2½ inches) long, on the baking sheets, leaving a space inbetween each. Put icing sugar above milk in ingredients list.

Bake in a preheated oven, 150°C (350°F), Gas Mark 2, for about 45 minutes until crisp, rotating the baking sheets halfway through cooking. Transfer to a wire rack to cool. Beat the mascarpone in a bowl with the icing sugar, milk and vanilla bean paste until smooth. Turn into a small bowl. Serve with the meringue fingers for dipping.

For pistachio & white chocolate meringues,
remove the skins from 50 g (2 oz) shelled pistachios (see page 70). Finely chop the pistachios and reserve. Make the meringues as above, using extra caster sugar to replace the muscovado sugar. Sprinkle with the nuts before baking. Gently heat 100 ml (3½ fl oz) double cream in a small saucepan with 100 g (3½ oz) chopped white chocolate until hot but not boiling. Remove from the heat and leave until the chocolate has melted. Leave to cool, then use to sandwich the fingers together.

redcurrant meringue cupcakes

Makes **16**
Preparation time **30 minutes**,
  plus cooling
Cooking time **20 minutes**

65 g (2½ oz) **lightly salted butter**, softened
165 g (6 oz) **caster sugar**
65 g (2½ oz) **self-raising flour**, sifted
1 **egg**
1 piece of **preserved stem ginger in syrup**, finely chopped
3 tablespoons **redcurrant jelly**
2 teaspoons **water**
75 g (3 oz) **redcurrants**, plus extra sprigs to decorate
2 **egg whites**
100 g (3½ oz) **caster sugar**

Place 16 mini silicone muffin cases on a baking sheet. Put the butter, 65 g (2½ oz) of the sugar, the flour, egg and ginger in a bowl and beat with a hand-held electric whisk until light and creamy. Divide among the cases.

Bake in a preheated oven, 180°C (350°F), Gas Mark 4, for 10–12 minutes until risen and just firm. Leave to cool in the cases for 2 minutes, then transfer to a wire rack to cool completely. Increase the oven temperature to 230°C (450°F), Gas Mark 8.

Heat the redcurrant jelly in a small saucepan with the measurement water until the jelly softens. Add the redcurrants and cook gently for 5 minutes to soften. Leave to cool.

Use a teaspoon to scoop out the centres of the cupcakes to make a cavity. Spoon the redcurrant mixture into the centres.

Whisk the egg whites in a thoroughly clean bowl until stiffly peaking. Gradually whisk in the remaining sugar, a dessertspoonful at a time and whisking well between each addition, until the mixture is stiff and glossy. Pile the meringue onto the cakes and swirl with a palette knife. Return to the baking sheet and bake for about 2 minutes, watching closely, until the meringue peaks are turning deep brown. Serve warm or cold decorated with small redcurrant sprigs.

For lemon meringue cupcakes, make the cakes as above, replacing the ginger with the finely grated rind of 1 lemon. Once cooled, scoop out the centres with a teaspoon and fill with a teaspoonful of lemon curd. Make the meringue and finish as above.

mini chocolate meringues

Makes **36**
Preparation time **15 minutes**,
   plus cooling
Cooking time 1 ¼ **hours**

butter, for greasing
3 **egg whites**
75 g (3 oz) **golden caster
   sugar**
75 g (3 oz) **light muscovado
   sugar**
75 g (3 oz) **milk chocolate**,
   grated

Grease and line 2 baking sheets with nonstick baking paper.

Whisk the egg whites in a thoroughly clean bowl until stiffly peaking. Whisk in the golden caster sugar 1 tablespoon at a time, then whisk in the light muscovado sugar, also 1 tablespoon at a time. Fold in the chocolate. Drop teaspoonfuls of the meringue mixture onto the baking sheets.

Bake in a preheated oven, 140°C (275°F), Gas Mark 1, for 1 ¼ hours, then turn off the heat and leave in the oven for another 30 minutes. Once cooled, gently peel away the paper from the meringues and store in paper cases in an airtight container for up to 3 days.

For white chocolate & mint discs, make up the meringue as above, but use 150 g (5 oz) golden caster sugar instead of the mixed caster and muscovado sugar. Fold in 75 g (3 oz) grated white chocolate in place of the milk chocolate and add 1 teaspoon mint extract. Place about 36 teaspoonfuls of the mixture on the baking sheets and spread with the back of the spoon to make shallow discs about 5 mm (¼ inch) thick. Bake as above.

baby passionfruit pavlovas

Makes **20**
Preparation time **30 minutes**,
  plus cooling
Cooking time **1 hour**

butter, for greasing
3 **egg whites**
175 g (6 oz) **caster sugar**
1 teaspoon **white wine**
  vinegar
1 teaspoon **cornflour**
6 **passionfruit**
150 ml (¼ pint) **double cream**
100 g (3½ oz) **Greek yogurt**
20 **physalis**

Grease and line 2 baking sheets with nonstick baking paper. Whisk the egg whites in a thoroughly clean bowl until stiffly peaking. Gradually whisk in the sugar, a dessertspoonful at a time, whisking well between each addition, until the mixture is stiff and glossy. Drizzle the vinegar into the bowl and sift in the cornflour. Stir gently.

Place 20 spoonfuls of the mixture, each about the size of a golf ball, on the lined baking sheets and flatten into a neat dome shape with a palette knife. Push a deep cavity into each centre using the back of a teaspoon. Bake in a preheated oven, 140°C (325°F), Gas Mark 1, for about 1 hour until crisp to the touch. Leave to cool on the baking sheets.

Scoop the pulp from 3 of the passionfruit and press through a sieve into a bowl. Add the cream and yogurt and whisk with a hand-held electric whisk until softly peaking. Spoon into the meringue cases. Scoop the pulp from the remaining passionfruit and spoon over the tops. Decorate each pavlova with a physalis.

For strawberry & vanilla pavlovas, split a vanilla pod lengthways and scoop out the seeds with the tip of a knife. (Halve the pod and put in a jar of caster sugar for 2–3 weeks, stirring occasionally, to make vanilla sugar.) Mash the seeds with 1 tablespoon caster sugar. Make the meringues as above, adding the vanilla sugar with the rest of the sugar. Bake as above. Fill the meringues with 150 ml (¼ pint) whipped double cream and scatter with small halved strawberries. Melt 3 tablespoons redcurrant jelly in a pan with 2 teaspoons water to dissolve. Drizzle over the strawberries to glaze.

banoffee meringues

Makes **20**
Preparation time **30 minutes**,
   plus cooling
Cooking time 1¼ **hours**

butter, for greasing
3 **egg whites**
100 g (3½ oz) **light
   muscovado sugar**
75 g (3 oz) **caster sugar**
1 small ripe **banana**
1 tablespoon **lemon juice**
150 ml (¼ pint) **double cream**
4 tablespoons **ready-made
   toffee fudge sauce**

Grease 2 baking sheets. Line with nonstick baking paper. Whisk the egg whites in a very clean bowl until stiffly peaking. Gradually whisk in the sugars, a teaspoonful at a time, until it has all been added. Whisk for a few minutes more until the mixture is thick and glossy. Take a large teaspoonful of meringue and, using another spoon to scoop off the first spoon, drop it onto the baking sheet to make an oval-shaped meringue. Continue until the mixture is used: making 40 meringues.

Bake in a preheated oven, 110°C (225°F), Gas Mark ¼ for 1–1¼ hours or until meringues are firm and may be easily peeled off the paper. Leave to cool on the paper.

Mash the banana roughly with the lemon juice. Whip the cream until it forms soft peaks, then whisk in 2 tablespoons of the toffee fudge sauce. Combine with the banana, then use to sandwich the meringues together and arrange in paper cake cases. Drizzle with the remaining toffee fudge sauce and serve. Store unfilled meringues in an airtight tin for up to 3 days.

For homemade toffee sauce, put 5 tablespoons water in a small heavy-based saucepan with 200 g (7 oz) caster sugar and heat gently until the sugar dissolves completely. Bring to the boil and boil until the syrup turns a golden caramel colour. Remove from the heat and dip the base of the pan in cold water to prevent further cooking. Add 50 g (2 oz) unsalted butter and 150 ml (¼ pint) double cream and return to a gentle heat, stirring until the caramel has softened and the sauce becomes smooth. Leave to cool. This sauce may be refrigerated for up to 5 days.

pistachio & chocolate meringues

Makes **16**
Preparation time **30 minutes**
Cooking time **1 hour**

butter, for greasing
3 **egg whites**
175 g (6 oz) **caster sugar**
50 g (2 oz) **shelled pistachio
nuts**, finely chopped
150 g (5 oz) **plain dark
chocolate**, broken into
pieces
150 ml (¼ pint) **double cream**

Grease and line 2 baking sheets with nonstick baking paper.

Whisk the egg whites in a very clean bowl until stiffly peaking. Gradually whisk in the sugar, a teaspoonful at a time, until it has all been added. Whisk for a few minutes more until the mixture is thick and glossy.

Fold in the pistachios, then spoon heaped teaspoonfuls of the mixture into rough swirly mounds on the baking sheets.

Bake in a preheated oven, 110°C (225°F), Gas Mark ¼, for 45–60 minutes, or until the meringues are firm and may be easily peeled off the paper. Leave to cool on the baking sheets.

Melt the chocolate (see page 14). Lift the meringues off the paper and dip the bases into the chocolate. Return to the paper, tilted on their sides, and leave in a cool place until the chocolate has hardened.

Whip the cream until just holding its shape, then use to sandwich the meringues together in pairs. Arrange in paper cake cases, if liked, on a cake plate or stand. Eat on the day they are filled. (Left plain, the meringues will keep in an airtight tin for 3 days.)

For saffron meringues with clotted cream, make the meringues as above, omitting the pistachio nuts and crumbling ½ teaspoon saffron strands into the meringue mixture when you start adding the sugar. Place dessertspoonfuls of the mixture onto the baking sheets and bake as above. Serve with a bowl of clotted cream.

french macaroons

Makes **24**
Preparation time **20 minutes**,
   plus standing
Cooking time **10 minutes**

butter, for greasing
50 g (2 oz) **icing sugar**
65 g (2½ oz) **ground
   almonds**
2 **egg whites**
100 g (3½ oz) **caster sugar**
pink and **green food
   colouring**

Grease and line 2 baking sheets with nonstick baking paper.

Put the icing sugar in a food processor with the ground almonds and blend to a very fine consistency.

Put the egg whites in a thoroughly clean bowl and whisk until stiffly peaking. Gradually whisk in the caster sugar, a tablespoonful at a time and whisking well after each addition, until thick and very glossy. Divide the mixture equally between 2 bowls and add a few drops of food colouring to each bowl. Divide the almond mixture equally between the 2 bowls and use a metal spoon to stir the mixtures gently to combine.

Place 1 colour in a piping bag fitted with a 1 cm (½ inch) plain nozzle and pipe 12 x 3 cm (1¼ inch) rounds onto 1 baking sheet. Tap the baking sheet firmly to smooth the surfaces of the macaroons. Wash and dry the bag and piping nozzle and pipe 12 rounds in the second colour onto the other baking sheet. Leave to stand for 30 minutes.

Bake in a preheated oven, 160°C (325°F), Gas Mark 3, for about 15 minutes, or until the surfaces feel crisp. Leave to cool before carefully peeling away the paper.

rich chocolate macaroons

Makes **12**
Preparation time **20 minutes**,
  plus standing and cooling
Cooking time **20 minutes**

50 g (2 oz) **icing sugar**
50 g (2 oz) **ground almonds**
4 tablespoons **cocoa powder**
2 **egg whites**
100 g (3 ½ oz) **caster sugar**

Filling
5 tablespoons **double cream**
100 g (3 ½ oz) **plain dark
  chocolate**, chopped

Line 2 baking sheets with nonstick baking paper. Put the icing sugar in a food processor with the ground almonds and cocoa powder and blend to a very fine consistency.

Put the egg whites in a thoroughly clean bowl and whisk until peaking. Gradually whisk in the caster sugar, a tablespoonful at a time and whisking well after each addition, until thick and very glossy. Add the almond mixture to the bowl and use a metal spoon to stir the ingredients together to combine.

Place in a piping bag fitted with a 1 cm (½ inch) plain nozzle and pipe 24 x 3 cm (1 ¼ inch) rounds onto the baking sheets. Tap the baking sheet firmly to smooth the surfaces of the macaroons slightly, then leave to stand for 30 minutes. Bake in a preheated oven, 160°C (325°F), Gas Mark 3, for about 15 minutes or until the surfaces feel crisp. Leave to cool before carefully peeling away the paper.

Heat the cream in a small saucepan until bubbling up around the edges but not boiling. Remove from the heat and stir in the chopped chocolate. Leave the chocolate to melt, stirring frequently, until smooth. Once the chocolate is cool and thickened enough to hold its shape, use to sandwich the macaroons together in pairs. Keep in a cool place until ready to serve.

For chocolate raspberry ganache, to serve with the macaroons, melt 100 g (3 ½ oz) chocolate (see page 15) with 5 tablespoons double cream. Add 1 tablespoon unsalted butter and 100 g (3 ½ oz) fresh raspberries. Heat gently over a low heat, stirring until butter is melted. Let stand at room temperature until cool and thickened.

almond & white chocolate kisses

Makes **18**
Preparation time **25 minutes**,
  plus cooling
Cooking time **15 minutes**

100 g (3½ oz) **unsalted
  butter**, softened, plus extra
  for greasing
100 g (3½ oz) **blanched
  almonds**
100 g (3½ oz) **golden caster
  sugar**
50 g (2 oz) **plain flour**, plus
  extra for dusting
50 g (2 oz) **self-raising flour**

Filling
100 g (3½ oz) **white
  chocolate**, chopped
25 g (1 oz) **unsalted butter**

Grease 2 baking sheets.

Put the almonds in a food processor and blend until
finely ground. Add the butter and sugar, sift in the flours
and blend until the mixture starts to come together.

Turn out onto a lightly floured surface and pat into a
smooth dough. Roll small balls of the dough, about the
size of a cherry and space on the baking sheets.

Bake in a preheated oven, 180°C (350°F), Gas Mark
4, for about 15 minutes until risen, cracked and pale
golden. Transfer to a wire rack to cool.

Make the chocolate filling by melting the chocolate and
butter in a saucepan. Use to sandwich the macaroons
together in pairs.

For gluten-free almond macaroons, grease and
line a large baking sheet with nonstick baking paper.
Whisk 2 egg whites until peaking and gradually whisk in
100 g (3½ oz) caster sugar. Stir in 125 g (4 oz) ground
almonds. Place small dessertspoonfuls, spaced slightly
apart, on the baking sheet and press a blanched almond
onto the top of each. Bake as above.

frosted chocolate whoopies

Makes 12–14
Preparation time **20 minutes**,
    plus cooling
Cooking time **15 minutes**

butter, for greasing
150 g (5 oz) **self-raising flour**
¼ teaspoon **bicarbonate of
    soda**
25 g (1 oz) **cocoa powder**
100 g (3 ½ oz) **golden caster
    sugar**
2 tablespoons **vanilla sugar**
    (see page 168)
1 **egg**
3 tablespoons **vegetable oil**
1 tablespoon **milk**
50 g (2 oz) **plain** or **milk
    chocolate**, chopped

Filling
100 g (3½ oz) **cream cheese**
2 tablespoons **icing sugar**,
    sifted
1 teaspoon finely grated
    orange rind
few drops of **orange extract**
    (optional)

Grease a large baking sheet.

Put the flour, bicarbonate of soda, cocoa powder and sugars in a bowl. Beat the egg with the vegetable oil and milk and add to the dry ingredients. Beat together to form a thick paste, adding a little more milk if the mixture feels crumbly.

Take teaspoonfuls of the mixture and roll into balls, about the size of a cherry, using floured hands. Space well apart on the baking sheet and flatten slightly.

Bake in a preheated oven, 200°C (400°F), Gas Mark 6, for 12 minutes until the mixture has spread and is pale golden. Transfer to a wire rack to cool.

Make the frosting by beating together the cream cheese, icing sugar, orange rind and extract, if using. Use to sandwich the cakes together. Melt the chocolate (see page 14) and spread over the tops of the whoopies.

For mascarpone & ginger frosting, to use as an alternative, finely chop 1 piece of drained stem ginger from a jar. Beat 100g (3½ oz) mascarpone cheese in a bowl with 15g (½oz) softened unsalted butter and 3 tablespoons golden icing sugar. Stir in the ginger until evenly mixed and use to sandwich the whoopies together. Spread the tops with melted white chocolate instead of the plain or milk.

vanilla & peanut whoopies

Makes **12–14**
Preparation time **20 minutes**,
   plus cooling
Cooking time **12 minutes**

butter, for greasing
175 g (6 oz) **self-raising
   flour**, sifted
¼ teaspoon **bicarbonate of
   soda**
100 g (3½ oz) **golden caster
   sugar**
2 tablespoons **vanilla sugar**
   (see page 168)
1 **egg**
3 tablespoons **vegetable oil**
1 tablespoon **milk**

Filling
5 tablespoons **smooth
   peanut butter**
25 g (1 oz) **lightly salted
   butter**, softened
3 tablespoons **icing sugar**,
   sifted
1 teaspoon hot **water**

Grease a large baking sheet.

Put the flour, bicarbonate of soda and sugars in a bowl. Beat the egg with the vegetable oil and milk and add to the dry ingredients.

Beat together to form a thick paste, adding a little more milk if the mixture feels crumbly.

Take teaspoonfuls of the mixture and roll into balls, about the size of a cherry, using floured hands. Space well apart on the baking sheet and flatten slightly.

Bake in a preheated oven 200°C (400°F), Gas Mark 6, for 12 minutes until the mixture has spread and is pale golden. Transfer to a wire rack to cool.

Make the filling by beating together the peanut butter, butter and icing sugar until smooth. Add the measurement hot water and beat until light and fluffy. Use to sandwich the cakes together.

For spiced whoopies with brandy butter, make the whoopies as above, adding 1 teaspoon ground mixed spice with the flour. Beat 75g (3oz) softenend unsalted butter in a bowl with 25g (1oz) icing sugar and 3 tablespoons brandy until smooth and creamy. Use to sandwich the whoopies together and serve dusted with icing sugar.

scones
& other
mini cakes

lavender tea scones

Makes **24**
Preparation time **20 minutes**,
  plus cooling
Cooking time **10 minutes**

40 g (1½ oz) chilled **butter**,
  diced, plus extra for greasing
225 g (7½ oz) **self-raising
  flour**, plus extra for dusting
1 teaspoon **baking powder**
4 **lavender flower stems**
150 ml (¼ pint) **buttermilk**
milk or **beaten egg**, to glaze
caster sugar, for dusting

Filling
150 ml (¼ pint) **double cream**
4 tablespoons **strawberry jam**

Grease a baking sheet.

Sift the flour and baking powder into a food processor. Pull the lavender flowers from the stems and add to the bowl with the butter. Blend until the mixture resembles breadcrumbs. Add the buttermilk and blend briefly to make a soft dough.

Turn out onto a lightly floured surface and roll out to 1.5 cm (¾ inch) thick. Cut out 24 rounds using a 3 cm (1¼ inch) round cutter, rerolling the trimmings as necessary. Transfer to the baking sheet, brush with milk or beaten egg and sprinkle with caster sugar.

Bake in a preheated oven, 220°C (425°F), Gas Mark 7, for 8-10 minutes until risen and pale golden. Transfer to a wire rack to cool.

Whip the cream until just holding its shape. Split the scones and sandwich with the jam and whipped cream.

For cranberry & orange scones, chop 50 g (2 oz) dried cranberries into small pieces and steep in 2 tablespoons orange juice until the orange is absorbed. Make the scones as above, adding ¼ teaspoon ground mixed spice with the flour and the cranberries and the finely grated rind of 1 small orange with the milk. Serve warm, split and buttered.

open saffron & blueberry scones

Makes **32**
Preparation time **15 minutes**,
plus cooling
Cooking time **10 minutes**

40 g (1½ oz) chilled **butter**,
diced, plus extra for greasing
about 150 ml (¼ pint) **milk**
½ teaspoon **saffron strands**
225 g (7½ oz) **self-raising
flour**, plus extra for dusting
1 teaspoon **baking powder**
200 g (7 oz) **clotted cream**
125 g (4 oz) **blueberries**
vanilla sugar (see page 168),
to sprinkle

Grease a baking sheet.

Heat half the milk in a small saucepan. Crumble in the saffron strands and remove from the heat. Leave to cool.

Sift the flour and baking powder into a food processor and add the butter. Blend until the mixture resembles breadcrumbs. Add the saffron milk and most of the remaining milk and blend briefly to make a soft dough, adding a little more milk if the dough feels dry.

Turn out onto a lightly floured surface and roll out to 1.5 cm (¾ inch) thick. Cut into 16 squares using a 3 cm (1¼ inch) cutter, rerolling the trimmings as necessary, and place on the baking sheet.

Bake in a preheated oven, 220°C (425°F), Gas Mark 7, for 8–10 minutes until risen and pale golden. Transfer to a wire rack to cool.

Split the scones in half and spread the cut sides with clotted cream. Pile the blueberries on top and serve sprinkled with vanilla sugar.

For white chocolate scones with vanilla & ginger butter, make the scones as above, omitting the saffron and stirring in 50 g (2 oz) grated white chocolate before the milk. Bake as above. Chop a piece of preserved stem ginger in syrup and blend in a food processor with 75 g (3 oz) softened unsalted butter until smooth. Blend in 25 g (1 oz) sifted icing sugar and turn into a small dish. Serve with the scones.

sweet carrot & rosemary scones

Makes **22–24**
Preparation time **15 minutes**,
plus cooling
Cooking time **10 minutes**

50 g (2 oz) chilled **lightly
salted butter**, diced, plus
extra for greasing
225 g (7½ oz) **stoneground
spelt flour**, plus extra for
dusting
2 teaspoons **baking powder**
½ teaspoon **cream of tartar**
2 teaspoons finely chopped
rosemary
2 tablespoons **caster sugar**
125 g (7 oz) small **carrots**,
finely grated
100 ml (3½ fl oz) **milk**, plus
extra to glaze

To serve
mascarpone cheese
fruit jelly, such as crab apple,
apple or orange

Grease a baking sheet.

Sift the flour, baking powder and cream of tartar into
a food processor, tipping in the grains left in the sieve.
Stir in the rosemary and sugar. Add the butter and blend
until the mixture resembles breadcrumbs. Stir in the
grated carrots and milk and mix to a soft dough, adding
a dash more milk if the dough feels dry.

Turn out onto a lightly floured surface and roll out to
1.5 cm (¾ inch) thick. Cut out 22–24 rounds using
a 3 cm (1¼ inch) cutter, rerolling the trimmings as
necessary. Transfer to the baking sheet and brush
with milk to glaze.

Bake in a preheated oven, 220°C (425°F), Gas Mark 7,
for 8-10 minutes until risen and pale golden. Transfer to
a wire rack to cool.

Split the scones and serve spread with mascarpone
and fruit jelly.

For wholemeal apple & sultana scones, mix 125 g
(4 oz) wholemeal flour, 100 g (3½ oz) self-raising flour,
1 teaspoon ground mixed spice and 2 teaspoons baking
powder in a bowl. Add 40 g (1½ oz) salted butter, cut
into small pieces, and rub in with the fingertips until
the mixture resembles breadcrumbs. Stir in 50 g
(2 oz) chopped sultanas and 1 peeled, cored and grated
dessert apple. Stir in 125 ml (4 fl oz) milk and mix to a
soft dough, adding a little more milk if the dough feels
dry. Roll out, shape and bake as above.

chocolate iced fancies

Makes **16**
Preparation time **45 minutes**,
   plus cooling
Cooking time **25 minutes**

100 g (3½ oz) **lightly salted
   butter**, softened, plus extra
   for greasing
125 g (4 oz) **plain dark
   chocolate**, chopped
125 g (4 oz) **light muscovado
   sugar**
2 **eggs**
50 g (2 oz) **self-raising flour**
25 g (1 oz) **cocoa powder**
50 g (2 oz) **ground almonds**
5 tablespoons **chocolate
   hazelnut spread**

Icing
200 g (7 oz) **plain dark
   chocolate**, chopped
2 tablespoons **golden syrup**
15 g (½ oz) **lightly salted
   butter**
50 g (2 oz) **milk chocolate**,
   chopped

Grease and line a 15 cm (6 inch) square tin with nonstick baking paper. Grease the paper.

Melt the chocolate (see page 14). Beat together the butter and sugar in a bowl until pale and creamy. Gradually beat in the eggs, adding a little flour to prevent the mixture curdling. Stir in the melted chocolate.

Sift the flour and cocoa powder over the bowl. Add the ground almonds and stir in gently. Turn into the tin and level the surface. Bake in a preheated oven, 160°C (325°F), Gas Mark 3, for about 20 minutes until risen and just firm to the touch. Transfer to a wire rack to cool.

Cut the cake into 16 squares and, using a palette knife, spread a little mound of chocolate hazelnut spread on the top of each one. Make the icing by melting the plain dark chocolate with the syrup and butter until smooth and glossy. Separately melt the milk chocolate. Spoon a little of the plain chocolate mixture over each cake and spread around the sides with a palette knife. Using a teaspoon, drizzle lines of milk chocolate over each cake.

For white chocolate fancies, make, bake and cut the cake as above, using melted white chocolate instead of dark chocolate and adding an extra 25 g (1 oz) self-raising flour to replace the cocoa powder. Use white chocolate spread instead of the chocolate hazelnut spread. Make the chocolate covering, using white chocolate instead of the plain, and use it to cover the cakes. Beat 50 g (2 oz) sifted icing sugar in a bowl with enough water to give a consistency that thickly coats the back of the spoon. Add a drop of pink food colouring. Drizzle lines over the cakes.

sweet potato mini loaves

Makes **10**
Preparation time **20 minutes**,
 plus cooling
Cooking time about **35
 minutes**

75 g (3 oz) **lightly salted
 butter**, softened, plus extra
 for greasing
200 g (7 oz) **sweet potato**,
 scrubbed and diced
75 g (3 oz) **light muscovado
 sugar**
1 teaspoon **vanilla extract**
1 **egg**
150 g (5 oz) **self-raising
 flour**, sifted
½ teaspoon **ground
 cinnamon**
½ teaspoon **baking powder**
4 tablespoons **flaked
 almonds**, lightly crushed
50g (2 oz) **white chocolate**,
 chopped

Grease 10 mini loaf tins or sections of a loaf tray, each with a capacity of about 60 ml (2½ fl oz).

Cook the sweet potato in a small saucepan of boiling water for 10–15 minutes until just tender. Drain and mash. Leave to cool.

Put the butter, sugar, vanilla extract, egg and sweet potato in a bowl, sift in the flour, cinnamon and baking powder, and beat with a hand-held electric whisk until smooth and creamy. Divide among the tins and place on a baking sheet. Scatter with the flaked almonds.

Bake in a preheated oven, 160°C (325°F), Gas Mark 3, for about 20 minutes until just firm to the touch. Leave in the tins for 5 minutes, then transfer to a wire rack to cool.

Melt the white chocolate (see page 14) and spoon over the tops of the cakes.

For parsnip, ginger & hazelnut cakes, cook and mash 175 g (6 oz) parsnips. Make the cake mixture as above, using the parsnip mash instead of the sweet potato mash and using 1 teaspoon ground ginger instead of the cinnamon. Before baking, sprinkle with 25 g (1 oz) chopped hazelnuts.

honeyed fig cakes

Makes **10**
Preparation time **20 minutes**
Cooking time **15 minutes**

100 g (3½ oz) **lightly salted butter**, softened, plus extra for greasing
100 g (3½ oz) **caster sugar**
2 **eggs**
100 g (3½ oz) **ground almonds**
½ teaspoon **almond extract**
25 g (1 oz) **self-raising flour**, sifted
finely grated rind of 1 **lemon**
3 **figs**, quartered
3 tablespoons **clear honey**
1½ tablespoons **lemon juice**

Grease and line the bases of 10 dariole moulds, each with a capacity of 100 ml (3½ fl oz), with circles of greaseproof paper.

Put the butter, sugar, eggs, ground almonds, almond extract, flour and lemon rind in a bowl and beat with a hand-held electric whisk until smooth and creamy. Divide among the dariole moulds. Rest a fig quarter on the centre of each sponge mixture.

Bake in a preheated oven, 200°C (400°F), Gas Mark 6, for about 15 minutes until just firm. Leave to cool in the moulds, then loosen the edges and transfer to a plate.

Mix together the honey and lemon juice and spoon over the figs.

For prune & walnut cups, grind 100 g (3½ oz) walnut pieces in a food processor or blender until finely ground. Make the sponge mixture as above, using the ground walnuts to replace the ground almonds and adding 50 g (2 oz) finely chopped prunes. Bake as above and serve topped with clotted cream and a drizzle of the honey and lemon juice.

strawberry rose shortcakes

Makes **12**
Preparation time **25 minutes**,
   plus cooling
Cooking time **22 minutes**

125 g (4 oz) **lightly salted
   butter**, softened, plus extra
   for greasing
50 g (2 oz) **caster sugar**
1 **egg**, beaten
1 teaspoon **vanilla extract**
125 g (4 oz) **self-raising flour**
½ teaspoon **baking powder**

Topping
3 tablespoons **redcurrant jelly**
2 teaspoons **water**
150 ml (¼ pint) **double cream**
1 tablespoon **icing sugar**,
   sifted
4 teaspoons **rosewater**
150 g (5 oz) small
   strawberries, halved

Grease 12 mini brioche moulds, each with a capacity of
40–50 ml (1¾–2 fl oz).

Beat together the butter and caster sugar until light
and fluffy. Gradually beat in the egg and vanilla extract,
adding a little flour to prevent the mixture curdling. Sift
the flour and baking powder into the bowl and stir in
gently. Divide among the moulds and level the surfaces.

Bake in a preheated oven, 180°C (350°F), Gas Mark 4,
for 20 minutes until just firm to the touch. Leave for 5
minutes, then transfer to a wire rack to cool.

Make the topping by putting the redcurrant jelly in
a small saucepan with the measurement water and
heating gently until the jelly has dissolved. Turn into a
small dish. Whip the cream with the icing sugar and
rosewater until just holding its shape. Spoon on top of
the shortcakes and decorate with strawberry halves.
Drizzle with the redcurrant syrup.

For blackcurrant cassis shortcakes, make the
shortcake mixture as above, adding ¼ teaspoon
ground mixed spice to the mixture. Divide between
mini muffin or tartlet tins, each section with a capacity
of about 50 ml (2 fl oz). Bake as above. Invert onto a
plate, skewer several holes into the centre of each and
spoon over 1 teaspoon of cassis liqueur so it seeps
into the shortcake. Whip 150 ml (¼ pint) double cream
with 2 tablespoons sifted icing sugar and pipe onto the
shortcakes. Arrange a cluster of blackcurrants on top
of each and spoon over a little warmed and strained
blackcurrant jam.

banana flapjack bites

Makes **16**
Preparation time **20 minutes**,
   plus cooling
Cooking time **15 minutes**

100 g (3½ oz) **lightly salted
   butter**
100 g (3½ oz) **golden syrup**
25 g (1 oz) **light muscovado
   sugar**
200 g (7 oz) **porridge oats**
1 ripe **banana**
1 teaspoon **lemon** or **lime
   juice**
150 ml (¼ pint) **double cream**
maple syrup, to drizzle

Place 16 mini silicone muffin cases on a baking sheet.

Put the butter, syrup and sugar in a small saucepan and heat gently until the butter has melted. Stir in the oats until combined. Divide among the cases and press down gently with the back of a dampened teaspoon.

Bake in a preheated oven, 180°C (350°F), Gas Mark 4, for 12 minutes, or until just beginning to colour around the edges. Leave in the cases for 10 minutes, then transfer to a wire rack to cool.

Mash the banana with the lemon or lime juice until puréed. Press the purée through a sieve into a bowl, scraping off the purée that clings to the underside of the sieve. Add the cream and whisk until the mixture holds its shape.

Spoon the banana cream over the flapjacks. Drizzle with a little maple syrup just before serving.

For coconut & ginger flapjacks, make the flapjack mixture as above, replacing 50 g (2 oz) of the oats with 50 g (2 oz) desiccated coconut and adding 1 finely chopped piece of preserved stem ginger in syrup. After baking, whip 150 ml (¼ pint) double cream with 2 tablespoons of the ginger syrup. Spoon onto the cakes and decorate with coconut shavings.

bite-sized vanilla sponges

Makes **10**
Preparation time **20 minutes**,
  plus cooling
Cooking time **15 minutes**

75 g (3 oz) **lightly salted
  butter**, softened
75 g (3 oz) **caster sugar**
75 g (3 oz) **self-raising flour**,
  sifted
1 **egg**, plus 1 **egg yolk**
1 teaspoon **vanilla bean
  paste**
icing sugar, for dusting

Filling
150 ml (¼ pint) **double cream**
5 tablespoons **strawberry** or
  raspberry jam

Put the butter, sugar, flour, egg, egg yolk and vanilla bean paste in a bowl and beat with a hand-held electric whisk until light and creamy. Divide among 10 sections of a 12-hole mini muffin tin.

Bake in a preheated oven, 180°C (350°F), Gas Mark 4, for about 15 minutes until risen and just firm. Leave in the tray for 5 minutes, then transfer to a wire rack to cool.

Split the cakes in half horizontally. Whip the cream until just holding its shape. Use the jam and cream to sandwich the cakes together. Serve dusted with icing sugar.

For poppy seed & orange splits, make the sponge mixture as above, adding 1 tablespoon poppy seeds and the finely grated rind of 1 orange. Split the cakes in half horizontally and sandwich together with 5 tablespoons orange curd. Blend 75 g (3 oz) sifted icing sugar with about 2 teaspoons orange juice to give a consistency that thickly coats the back of the spoon. Using a palette knife, gently spread the icing over the tops of the cakes.

lemon glazed cardamom madeleines

Makes **about 30**
Preparation time **20 minutes**,
   plus setting
Cooking time **30 minutes**

125 g (4 oz) **lightly salted
   butter**, melted, plus extra for
   greasing
125 g (4 oz) **self-raising
   flour**, plus extra for dusting
2 teaspoons **cardamom pods**
3 **eggs**
125 g (4 oz) **caster sugar**
finely grated rind of 1 **lemon**
½ teaspoon **baking powder**

Glaze
2 tablespoons **lemon juice**
75 g (3 oz) **icing sugar**, sifted,
   plus extra for dusting

Grease a madeleine tray with melted butter and dust with flour. Tap out the excess flour.

Crush the cardamom pods using a pestle and mortar to release the seeds. Remove the shells and crush the seeds a little further.

Put the eggs, caster sugar, lemon rind and crushed cardamom seeds in a heatproof bowl and rest the bowl over a saucepan of gently simmering water. Whisk with a hand-held electric whisk until the mixture is thick and pale and the mixture leaves a trail when lifted.

Sift the flour and baking powder into the bowl and gently fold in using a large metal spoon. Drizzle the melted butter around the edges of the mixture and fold the ingredients together to combine. Spoon the mixture into the madeleine sections until about two-thirds full. (Keep the remaining mixture for a second batch.)

Bake in a preheated oven, 220°C (425°F), Gas Mark 7, for about 10 minutes until risen and golden. Leave in the tray for 5 minutes, then transfer to a wire rack.

Make the glaze by putting the lemon juice in a bowl and beating in the icing sugar. Brush over the madeleines and leave to set. Serve lightly dusted with icing sugar.

For espresso madeleines with coffee glaze, mix 1 teaspoon instant espresso coffee powder with 2 teaspoons hot water. Make the madeleines, adding the coffee mixture once the whisk leaves a trail. Bake as above. Mix ½ teaspoon espresso coffee powder with 2 teaspoons hot water. Beat with 50 g (2 oz) sifted icing sugar until smooth and brush over the madeleines.

lamingtons

Makes **24**
Preparation time **20 minutes**,
 plus overnight standing
 and setting
Cooking time **30 minutes**

125 g (4 oz) **unsalted butter**,
 softened, plus extra for
 greasing
125 g (4 oz) **caster sugar**
2 **eggs**, lightly beaten
250 g (8 oz) **self-raising
 flour**, sifted
pinch of **salt**
4 tablespoons **milk**
1 teaspoon **vanilla extract**

Coating
400 g (13 oz) **icing sugar**
100 g (3½ oz) **cocoa powder**
150–175 ml (5–6 fl oz) boiling
 water
200 g (7 oz) **desiccated
 coconut**

Grease an 18 x 25 cm (7 x 10 inch) cake tin and base-line the base with nonstick baking paper.

Beat the butter and sugar together in a bowl until pale and creamy. Gradually beat in the eggs, adding a little flour to prevent the mixture curdling. Add the flour and salt and fold in with the milk and vanilla extract. Turn into the tin and level the surface.

Bake in a preheated oven, 190°C (375°F), Gas Mark 5, for 25-30 minutes until risen and firm to the touch. Leave to cool in the tin for 5 minutes, then loosen the edges, transfer to a wire rack and peel off the lining paper. Leave overnight, then cut into 24 squares.

Sift the icing sugar and cocoa powder into a bowl, making a well in the centre and beating in the boiling water to make a smooth icing with pouring consistency. Pour the desiccated coconut onto a plate. Use 2 forks to dip each cake into the icing and coat with the coconut. Leave to set on nonstick baking paper.

For cherry & almond splits, make the cake as above, adding 100 g (3½ oz) finely chopped sour dried cherries and 1 teaspoon almond extract. Once cooled, cut in half horizontally and sandwich together with 6 tablespoons cherry conserve, removing any large fruit pieces. Sift 200 g (7 oz) icing sugar into a bowl and mix in 5–6 teaspoons cold water to make a spreadable icing. Spread over the cake and scatter with toasted, crushed flaked almonds. Leave to firm up for 30 minutes, then cut into 24 squares.

treats for
kids

baby butterflies

Makes **16**
Preparation time **25 minutes**, plus cooling
Cooking time **12 minutes**

65 g (2½ oz) **lightly salted butter**, softened
65 g (2½ oz) **caster sugar**
65 g (2½ oz) **self-raising flour**, sifted
1 teaspoon **vanilla extract**
1 **egg**
icing sugar, for dusting

Buttercream
75 g (3 oz) **unsalted butter**, softened
100 g (3½ oz) **icing sugar**, sifted
pink food colouring
1 teaspoon hot **water**

Place 16 mini silicone muffin cases on a baking sheet.

Put the butter, sugar, flour, vanilla extract and egg in a bowl and beat with a hand-held electric whisk until light and creamy. Divide among the cases.

Bake in a preheated oven, 180°C (350°F), Gas Mark 4, for 10–12 minutes until risen and just firm. Leave to cool in the cases for 2 minutes then transfer to a wire rack to cool completely.

Make the buttercream by beating together the butter and icing sugar until combined. Add a little pink food colouring and the measurement water and beat until smooth and creamy.

Use a small, sharp knife to cut out circles from the tops of the cakes and cut the circles in half to shape butterfly wings. Put the buttercream in a piping bag fitted with a small star nozzle and use to pipe swirls into the scooped-out tops of the cakes. Position the butterfly wings on top and dust lightly with icing sugar.

For white chocolate frosting, melt 100 g (3½ oz) chopped white chocolate with 25 g (1 oz) unsalted butter in a microwave until no lumps remain. Remove from the heat and sift in 100 g (3½ oz) icing sugar. Stir well until combined. Use instead of the buttercream to spoon or pipe onto the cupcakes.

vanilla flowers

Makes **30**
Preparation time **30 minutes**
Cooking time **15 minutes**

200 g (7 oz) **butter**, softened,
   plus extra for greasing
few drops of **vanilla extract**
50 g (2 oz) **icing sugar**
175 g (6 oz) **plain flour**
50 g (2 oz) **cornflour**
cake decorations, to decorate

Grease and line 2 large baking sheets and line with nonstick baking paper.

Place the butter and vanilla extract in a mixing bowl and sift in the icing sugar. Beat together then sift in the flour and the cornflour a little at a time and fold in with a metal spoon.

Place in a piping bag fitted with a 1 cm (½ in) star nozzle and pipe the mixture onto the baking sheets, making 30 little flower shapes, spacing them slightly apart. To finish a flower, push the nozzle down into the piped flower as you stop squeezing. Press a decoration into the centre of each one.

Bake in a preheated oven, 190°C (375°F), Gas Mark 5, for 10–15 minutes, or until a pale golden colour. Leave for 2 minutes on the baking sheets then transfer to a wire rack to cool.

For chocolate sandwiches, make the biscuit mixture as above and put into a piping bag fitted with a 1 cm (½ inch) star nozzle. Pipe 3 thin lines of the mixture, each touching the previous line, to shape a rectangular biscuit measuring about 5 x 3 cm (2 x 1¼ inches). Repeat with the remaining mixture, spacing them slightly apart, making sure you end up with an even number. Bake as above. Melt 75 g (3 oz) milk chocolate (see page 14) and use to sandwich the biscuits together.

sweetie-topped cookie cakes

Makes **16**
Preparation time **15 minutes**,
  plus cooling
Cooking time **12 minutes**

50 g (2 oz**) unsalted butter**
2 tablespoons **golden syrup**
100 g (3½ oz) **porridge oats**
40 g (1½ oz) **desiccated
  coconut**
40 g (1½ oz) **dried
  cranberries**, chopped
50 g (2 oz) **icing sugar**, sifted
1½ teaspoons **water**
**mini sugar-coated chocolate
  beans**, to decorate

Place 16 mini silicone muffin cases on a baking sheet.

Put the butter and syrup in a small saucepan and heat gently until the butter has melted. Remove from the heat and stir in the porridge oats, coconut and cranberries. Beat well until evenly mixed, thendivide among the cases and press down gently.

Bake in a preheated oven, 190°C (375°F), Gas Mark 5, for about 12 minutes, or until turning golden around the edges. Leave to cool in the cases.

Beat the icing sugar with the measurement water and drizzle a little around the edges of the cakes. Gently press the chocolate beans into the icing.

For tangy yogurt frosting, line a sieve with 4 thicknesses of kitchen paper and spoon 100 g (3½ oz) Greek yogurt into the sieve. Bring up the edges of the paper and gently squeeze out the liquid from the yogurt until you have a thickened ball of yogurt. Tip into a bowl with 125 g (4 oz) sifted icing sugar and mix to form a soft frosting. Swirl over the cakes instead of using the icing and sweets.

puppies & kittens

Makes **20**
Preparation time **1 hour**, plus
 cooling
Cooking time **15 minutes**

butter, for greasing
1 quantity **Chocolate Sable
 Dough** (made by substituting
 25 g/1 oz flour with cocoa
 powder in the Vanilla Sable
 Dough, page 76)
flour, for dusting
175 g (6 oz) **pink ready-to-
 roll icing**
edible silver or **gold balls**
50 g (2 oz) **pale brown ready-
 to-roll icing**
175 g (6 oz) **blue ready-to-
 roll icing**
1 **tube** of **black writing icing**
175 g (6 oz) **chocolate-
 flavoured ready-to-roll
 icing**

Buttercream
75 g (3 oz) **icing sugar**, plus
 extra for dusting
50 g (2 oz) **lightly salted
 butter**, softened
1 teaspoon hot **water**

Grease a large baking sheet.

Roll out the cookie dough on a lightly floured surface
and cut out rounds using an 8 cm (3¼ inch) cookie
cutter, rerolling the trimmings to make 20 in all. Place
on the baking sheet, spacing them slightly apart.

Bake in a preheated oven, 180°C (350°F), Gas Mark 4,
for 15 minutes, or until beginning to darken around the
edges. Transfer to a wire rack to cool.

Make the buttercream by beating together the icing
sugar, butter and measurement water until smooth
and creamy. Place in a piping bag fitted with a fine plain
nozzle.

Make the kittens by shaping 10 triangular pieces of
pink icing for noses on a sugar-dusted surface. Secure
to the centres of half the cookies with buttercream.
Press 4 cm (1¾ inch) strips of pink icing to the base
of the cookies. Stud with silver or gold balls to make
collars. Shape pointed ears in pale brown icing and
secure with frosting. Pipe features onto the faces with
the buttercream, then add round eyes made of pale
brown icing and bow ties made of blue icing. With
the writing icing, draw a black line down the centre
of the eyes.

For puppies, shape 10 triangles of pale brown icing for
noses. Secure to the centres of the remaining cookies
with buttercream. Make collars in blue icing and stud
with silver or gold balls. Pipe features onto the faces
with the buttercream, then add ears, shaped from the
chocolate-flavoured icing, pink tongues and brown eyes.

magic wands

Makes **14**
Preparation time **25 minutes**,
  plus cooling and setting
Cooking time **15 minutes**

200 g (7 oz) **unsalted butter**,
  softened, plus extra for
  greasing
50 g (2 oz) **caster sugar**
250 g (8 oz) **plain flour**, sifted
1 teaspoon **vanilla extract**
a few drops each of **yellow**
  and **orange liquid food**
  colouring
150 g (5 oz) **royal icing**
  sugar, sifted
different-coloured sugar
  sprinkles
edible silver balls

Grease 2 baking sheets. Beat together the butter and sugar until very pale and creamy. Beat in the flour and vanilla extract until smooth.

Divide the cookie mixture in half and stir the yellow food colouring into one half and the orange colouring into the other. Put the cookie mixture into 2 large piping bags fitted with 1 cm (½ in) plain nozzles. Pipe fingers onto the baking sheets, each about 12 cm (5 inches) long, spacing them slightly apart.

Bake in a preheated oven, 180°C (350°F), Gas Mark 4, for 15 minutes, or until slightly risen and just beginning to darken. Leave to cool for 5 minutes, then transfer to a wire rack to cool completely.

Beat the royal icing sugar with enough water to give a consistency that just holds its shape. Spread a little icing over one end of each cookie and scatter with plenty of sugar sprinkles and silver balls. Leave in a cool place to set for about 1 hour.

For fun letter biscuits, make the cookie mixture as above, but without adding the food colouring. Place in a piping bag fitted with a 5 mm (¼ inch) plain nozzle. Use to pipe letter shapes, about 5 cm (2 inches) tall, onto the baking sheets. Bake as above. Decorate with tubes of colourful writing icing, securing small sweets or sugar sprinkles to decorate.

sticky chocolate orange cakes

Makes **16**
Preparation time **20 minutes**,
  plus cooling and setting
Cooking time **15 minutes**

65 g (2½ oz) **lightly salted
  butter**, softened
65 g (2½ oz) **caster sugar**
65 g (2½ oz) **self-raising
  flour**, sifted
finely grated rind of ½ **orange**
1 **egg**
6 tablespoons **orange
  marmalade**
2 teaspoons **water**
75 g (3 oz) **milk chocolate**,
  chopped

Place 16 mini silicone muffin cases on a baking sheet.

Put the butter, sugar, flour, orange rind and egg in a
bowl and beat with a hand-held electric whisk until light
and creamy. Divide among the cases.

Bake in a preheated oven, 180°C (350°F), Gas Mark 4,
for 10–12 minutes until risen and just firm. Leave in the
cases for 2 minutes then transfer to a wire rack to cool
completely.

Use a teaspoon to scoop out (and discard) a little
of the sponge from the top of each cake to make a
small cavity. Put the marmalade in a small saucepan
with the measurement water and heat gently until the
marmalade has melted. Leave to cool slightly, then
spoon a little onto the top of each cake. Leave to set.

Melt the chocolate (see page 14). Spoon onto the tops
of the cakes and spread gently to the edges.

For teatime strawberry cakes, make the cakes as
above, omitting the orange rind and adding 1 teaspoon
vanilla extract. After baking, remove the cakes from
the cases and split in half horizontally. Sandwich each
back together with 1 teaspoon strawberry-flavoured
fromage frais and a thin slice of strawberry. Dust the
tops with icing sugar.

wiggly worm

Serves **11**
Preparation time **45 minutes**, plus cooling
Cooking time **20 minutes**

150 g (5 oz) **lightly salted butter**, softened
150 g (5 oz) **caster sugar**
175 g (6 oz) **self-raising flour**, sifted
3 **eggs**
1 teaspoon **vanilla extract**
50 g (2 oz) **milk chocolate**, grated
icing sugar, for dusting
100 g (3½ oz) **pink** or **red ready-to-roll icing**
50 g (2 oz) **chocolate-flavoured ready-to-roll icing**
12 small **candy-covered chocolate sweets**

Buttercream
75 g (3 oz) **unsalted butter**, softened
125 g (4 oz) **icing sugar**, sifted

Line a 12-hole muffin tin with paper cake cases.

Put the butter, sugar, flour, eggs and vanilla extract in a bowl and beat with a hand-held electric whisk until smooth and creamy. Divide among the cases.

Bake in a preheated oven, 180°C (350°F), Gas Mark 4, for 20 minutes, or until risen and just firm to the touch. Transfer to a wire rack to cool.

Make the buttercream by beating together the butter and sugar in a bowl until smooth and creamy. Remove one cooled cake from its case and take a thick, angled slice off the top, and discard. Spread a little of the buttercream over another cake, position the slice on top and spread with buttercream to make a large 'face'.

Spread a large, rectangular board with 4 tablespoons of the buttercream and scatter with the grated chocolate. Spread the remaining buttercream over the cakes, then position in a snaking line over the chocolate, with the face cake at the front.

Roll out the pink or red icing thinly on a surface lightly dusted with icing sugar and cut out 9 rounds using a 5 cm (2 inch) cookie cutter. Place on all the cakes except the face and end cakes. Cut out a pointed tail from the trimmings and place on the end cake.

Roll out the chocolate icing and cut out a round using a slightly larger cutter. Position on the face cake. Then cut out 10 x 2.5 cm (1 inch) rounds. Place on the rest of the cakes and top each with a candy-covered chocolate sweet. Shape and position some eyes and a mouth with the icing trimmings and remaining sweets.

birthday cake stack

Makes **18**
Preparation time **25 minutes**,
  plus cooling
Cooking time **20 minutes**

175 g (6 oz) **lightly salted
  butter**, softened
175 g (6 oz) **golden caster
  sugar**
3 **eggs**
200 g (7 oz) **self-raising flour**
1 teaspoon **baking powder**
finely grated rind of 2 **lemons**

Buttercream
125 g (4 oz) **unsalted butter**,
  softened
200 g (7 oz) **icing sugar**,
  sifted
a few drops of **pink** or **blue
  food colouring** (optional)

To decorate
125 g (4 oz) **small sweets**,
  such as dolly mixtures and
  jellies
sugar sprinkles (optional)
birthday candles and
  candleholders

Line 18 sections of 2 x 12-hole bun trays with paper cake cases. Put the butter, caster sugar, eggs, flour, baking powder and lemon rind in a bowl and beat with a hand-held electric whisk for about 1 minute until light and creamy. Divide among the cases.

Bake in a preheated oven, 180°C (350°F), Gas Mark 4, for 20 minutes, or until risen and just firm to the touch. Transfer to a wire rack to cool.

Make the buttercream by beating together the unsalted butter and icing sugar in a bowl until smooth and creamy. Beat in the food colouring, if using. Spread the buttercream over the cakes using a small palette knife. Decorate the cakes with plenty of small sweets and sugar sprinkles, if using.

Arrange a layer of cakes on a serving plate and stack another 2 or 3 tiers on top to serve.

For christmas cake stack, make the cakes as above, using red, white or silver cases or a mixture of all three. Beat 75 g (3 oz) soft unsalted butter with 100 g (3½ oz) sifted icing sugar until light and fluffy, then spread over the cakes. Thinly roll out 150 g (5 oz) white ready-to-roll icing on a surface dusted with icing sugar and cut out rounds using a 6 cm (2½ inch) cutter. Position on top of the cakes. Roll out the white icing trimmings and 50 g (2 oz) red ready-to-roll icing and cut out star shapes in various sizes in both colours. Leave to set on nonstick baking paper, then arrange over the stacked cakes along with small candy canes and silver balls, secured to the white icing with dots of writing icing.

milk chocolate crackles

Makes **16**
Preparation time **10 minutes**,
plus setting
Cooking time **2 minutes**

200 g (7 oz) **milk chocolate,**
chopped
150 g (5 oz) **cornflakes**
coloured sugar sprinkles, to
decorate

Place 16 mini silicone muffin cases on a tray.

Melt the chocolate (see page 14). Using your hands,
crush the cornflakes until broken into very small flakes.
Tip into the chocolate and mix thoroughly until the
cornflakes are coated in a thin film of chocolate.

Use a teaspoon to scoop the mixture into the cases,
pressing it down firmly so the cakes will hold together
when set. Decorate with sugar sprinkles. Chill for about
1 hour until set.

For chocolate fridge cakes, melt 150 g (5 oz) milk
chocolate in a pan with 25 g (1 oz) unsalted butter,
stirring frequently until the mixture is smooth. Cut 25
g (1 oz) marshmallows into small pieces with scissors
and chop 25 g (1 oz) shortbread or digestive biscuits
into pieces no bigger than 1 cm (½ inch). Roughly
chop 8 natural glacé cherries. Add to the bowl and
mix until coated in chocolate. Divide among 16 mini
silicone muffin cases and scatter with white chocolate
shavings. Chill as above.

happy faces

Makes **16**
Preparation time **40 minutes**,
   plus chilling and cooling
Cooking time **15 minutes**

200 g (7 oz) chilled **unsalted butter**, diced, plus extra for greasing
275 g (9 oz) **plain flour**, plus extra for dusting
100 g (3½ oz) **icing sugar**, sifted
2 **egg yolks**
2 teaspoons **vanilla bean paste**
4 tablespoons **strawberry** or **raspberry jam**

Buttercream
125 g (4 oz) **icing sugar**
75 g (3 oz) **unsalted butter**, softened
1 teaspoon hot **water**

Grease 2 baking sheets.

Put the butter and flour in a food processor and blend until the mixture resembles breadcrumbs. Add the sugar, egg yolks and vanilla bean paste and blend to make a smooth dough. Wrap in clingfilm and chill for at least 1 hour.

Roll out the cookie dough on a lightly floured surface. Cut out rounds using a 6 cm (2½ inch) cookie cutter, rerolling the trimmings to make 16 in all. Place on the baking sheets, spaced slightly apart.

Cut out eyes in half the rounds, using a 1 cm (½ inch) cookie cutter or the end of a large, plain piping nozzle. Also cut out a large, smiling mouth, using a small, sharp knife or scalpel. Bake in a preheated oven, 180°C (350°F), Gas Mark 4, for 15 minutes, or until pale golden, then transfer to a wire rack to cool.

Make the buttercream by beating together the icing sugar, butter and measurement water until smooth and creamy. Spread the buttercream over the plain cookies, then spread with the jam. Gently press the face cookies on top.

For chocolate heart biscuits, make the dough as above, replacing 3 tablespoons of the flour with cocoa powder. Cut out heart shapes from the biscuit dough using a small cutter and bake as above. Once cooled, sandwich the biscuits together in pairs with white chocolate spread. Melt 50 g (2 oz) white chocolate and spoon into the corner of a small polythene bag. Snip off the merest tip and pipe an outline around the edges of the hearts.

little dinos

Makes **20**

Preparation time **1 hour**, plus chilling

Cooking time **15 minutes**

200 g (7 oz) chilled **unsalted butter**, diced, plus extra for greasing

275 g (9 oz) **plain flour**, plus extra for dusting

100 g (3½ oz) **icing sugar**

2 **egg yolks**

2 teaspoons **vanilla bean paste**

300 g (10 oz) **green ready-to-roll icing**

125 g (4 oz) **yellow ready-to-roll icing**

70 g (2¾ oz) **white chocolate rainbow buttons**

25 g (1 oz) **brown ready-to-roll icing**

Buttercream

125 g (4 oz) **icing sugar**, sifted

75 g (3 oz) **unsalted butter**, softened

1 teaspoon hot **water**

Grease 2 baking sheets. To make the dough put the butter and flour in a food processor and blend until the mixture resembles breadcrumbs. Add the sugar, egg yolks and vanilla and blend to a smooth dough. Wrap in clingfilm and chill the dough for at least 1 hour.

Roll out on a lightly floured surface and cut out rounds with a 10 cm (4 inch) cutter, rerolling the trimmings making 20. Cut each round in half and bake on baking sheets, in a preheated oven, 180°C (350°F), Gas Mark 4, for 15 minutes, until pale golden. Transfer to a wire rack.

Knead the green icing a little on a surface lightly dusted with icing sugar. Tear the yellow icing into pieces and dot over the green icing. Roll the lump of icing with your hands into a thick sausage. Fold it in half and roll again. Repeat rolling and folding until the colours have marbled together. Beat together the icing sugar and butter with the water until smooth and creamy. Put the buttercream in a piping bag with a fine plain nozzle. Roll out the marbled icing thinly. Lay a cookie over the icing and, using a small, sharp knife, cut around it, adding an icing tail.

Pipe buttercream over the cookie and lay the marbled icing on top. Repeat with the rest of the cookies. Reroll the icing trimmings and cut out small heads, marking mouths with a knife. Secure to the bodies with frosting. Shape and secure ears and feet. Cut the chocolate buttons into triangles and, using buttercream, secure along the top of each 'body', making the triangles smaller at the tail end. Pipe eyes and claws with buttercream. Shape and secure balls of brown icing for the centres of the eyes.

wise old owls

Makes **18**
Preparation time **1¼ hours**,
   plus cooling and setting
Cooking time **15 minutes**

butter, for greasing
1 quantity **Vanilla Cookie
   Dough**, chilled (see page
   230)
butter, for greasing
flour, for dusting
1 tablespoon **egg white**,
   lightly beaten
2 teaspoons **cocoa powder**
1 teaspoon **water**
150 g (5 oz) **royal icing
   sugar**, sifted
50 g (2 oz) each of **white,
   blue** and **yellow ready-to-
   roll icing**

Grease 2 baking sheets. Copy the owl picture opposite
to make a simple template about 5 cm (2 inches) high.

Roll out the cookie dough on a lightly floured surface.
Lay the template over the dough and, using a small,
sharp knife or scalpel, cut around it. Reroll the trimmings
to make 18 in all. Place on the baking sheets, spacing
them slightly apart.

Beat together the egg white, cocoa powder and
measurement water to make a smooth, thin paste. Using
a fine paintbrush, paint the wing, head and beak areas on
the owls. Bake in a preheated oven, 180°C (350°F), Gas
Mark 4, for 15 minutes, or until pale golden. Transfer to
a wire rack to cool.

Beat the royal icing sugar with enough water to give a
consistency that holds its shape. Put the royal icing in a
piping bag fitted with a fine plain nozzle. Use the white
ready-to-use icing to shape eyes, then secure them with
a little royal icing from the bag. Use the blue icing to
shape centres for the eyes, then secure with royal icing.
Cut out feet in yellow icing and secure. Use the icing left
in the bag to paint the wing and breast feathers. Leave
in a cool place to set for about 1 hour.

For trick or treat ghosties, roll out the dough as above
and cut out shapes using a ghost-shaped cutter. Bake
as above and leave to cool. Blend 200 g (7 oz) sifted
royal icing sugar with enough water to make a paste
that is spreadable but holds its shape. Using a palette
knife, spread the icing over the biscuits. Leave to set for
a couple of hours. Use a tube of black writing icing to
pipe eyes and smiling mouths.

window cookies

Makes **10**
Preparation time **10 minutes**, plus cooling
Cooking time **20 minutes**

1 quantity **Vanilla Cookie Dough**, chilled (see page 230)
flour, for dusting
175g (6 oz) **coloured boiled sweets**, lightly crushed
1 quantity **Royal Icing** (see page 15)
10 **chocolate flakes**
12 small **sugar-coated chocolates**
sugar sprinkles, to decorate

Line 2 baking sheets with nonstick baking paper. Roll out the cookie dough on a lightly floured surface. Cut out 10 x 8 cm (4 x 3¼ inches) rectangles and transfer to the baking sheets.

Cut out 4 squares from each rectangle to resemble window panes. Gather the trimmings and reroll the dough to make more window shapes. Place the windows on the baking sheets and put a boiled sweet in each cut out square.

Bake in a preheated oven at 180°C (350°F), Gas Mark 4 for 12 minutes or until the cookies begin to colour and the sweets have melted to fill the frames. If necessary ease the sweets into the corners with a toothpick. Leave to cool on the baking sheets. Place the icing in a piping bag fitted with a fine plain nozzle. Pipe a little icing onto the back of each flake bar and secure one flake along the base of each cookie. Make sure the chocolate sits straight along the bottom so it supports the cookie.

Add flower petals and trailing leaves around the windows, using the remaining icing in the bag. Before it sets, press small candies into the frames in the centres of the windows.

Leave to cool before carefully peeling away the paper.

index

almond extract: cherry
& almond splits 206
almonds:
  almond & polenta
    shortbreads 48
  almond & white
    chocolate kisses 178
  almond praline buns 130
  almond-coffee cake 116
  amaretti & almond
    mincemeat 46
  cherry bakewells 102
  chilli & cardamom
    morsels 72
  chocolate blondie bites
    100
  chocolate iced fancies
    192
  citrus baklava 144
  florentines 70
  gluten-free almond
    macaroons 178
  mini trifle cups 58
  stollen slice 114
amaretti biscuits:
  amaretti & almond
    mincemeat 46
  amaretti plum cakes 34
amaretto liqueur: amaretti
  & almond mincemeat 46
apples:
  blackberry & apple vol
    au vents 146
  cider-glazed apple slice
    106
  wholemeal apple &
    sultana scones 190
apricots:
  apricot & ginger cakes
    34
  apricot cheesecake
    bites 28
  apricot & orange simnel
    cakes 62

cardamom & apricot
  buns 122
hazelnut & apricot
  friands 22

baby shower cookies 94
bakewells: cherry bake-
  wells 102
baklava:
  baklava with spices 144
bananas:
  banana flapjack bites
    200
  banoffee meringues 170
  gluten-free banoffi bites
    52
beetroot: red velvet mini
  cakes 50
birthday bundles 86
birthday cake stack 224
biscotti: pistacho biscotti 84
biscuits:
  chocolate heart biscuits
    228
  chocolate thumbprint
    biscuits 68
  festive tree biscuits 90
  fun letter biscuits 218
  pink heart biscuits 92
  shoes & bags 92
blackberry & apple vol au
  vents 146
blackcurrant cassis
  shortcakes 198
blueberries:
  blueberry friands 22
  mini nectarine &
    blueberry tarts 154
  open saffron &
    blueberry scones 188
blueberry conserve:
  blueberry & cream
    cheese tartlets 140
boiled sweets: window
  cookies 234
Brazil nuts: mini Christmas
  cakes 64
Breton cake 110
brownies:

gluten-free chocolate
  brownies 100
real chocolate brownies
  124
buns:
  almond praline buns 130
  cardamom & apricot
    buns 122
  crème pâtissière buns
    130
  sour cherry buns 122
butterflies:
  baby butterflies 210
  walnut & muscovado
    butterflies 52
buttery Breton cake 110

candied peel:
  florentines 70
  stollen slice 114
caramel:
  caramel pecan sauce 30
  chocolate caramel
    shortbreads 48
  peanut caramel
    cupcakes 56
cardamom:
  cardamom & apricot
    buns 122
  chilli & cardamon
    morsels 72
  lemon & cardamom
    shortbreads 74
  lemon glazed cardamom
    madeleines 204
carrots:
  passion cake squares
    112
  sweet carrot & rosemary
    scones 190
cassis: blackcurrant cassis
  shortcakes 198
cheese:
  apricot cheesecake
    bites 28
  blueberry & cream
    cheese tartlets 140
  brown sugar meringues
    162

chocolate ginger
  cheesecakes 28
chocolate tiramisu cups
  58
mascarpone & ginger
  frosting 180
mascarpone & vanilla
  ice cream 154
pear & cream cheese
  triangles 136
plum tripiti 136
cherries:
  black forest bites 40
  cherry & almond splits
    206
  homemade cherry
    conserve 102
  sour cherry buns 122
cherries, glacé:
  cherry bakewells 102
  florentines 70
chilli powder: chilli &
  cardamon morsels 72
chillies: chilli polenta
  cakes 54
  fiery chocolate
    cupcakes 54
chocolate:
  almond & white
    chocolate kisses 178
  chocolate blondie bites
    100
  chocolate caramel
    shortbreads 48
  chocolate eclairs &
    cream liqueur 134
  chocolate filo twiglets
    152
  chocolate fridge cakes
    226
  frosted chocolate
    whoopies 180
  chocolate fudge
    cupcakes 30
  chocolate ginger
    cheesecakes 28
  chocolate iced
    fancies 192
  chocolate, orange &

walnut fudge 120
chocolate sandwiches 212
chocolate thumbprint biscuits 68
chocolate tiramisu cups 58
dark chocolate drops 82
double-choc nuggets 80
feathered chocolate profiteroles 148
florentines 70
glossy chocolate dip 78
glossy chocolate sauce 40
gluten-free chocolate brownies 100
milk chocolate crackles 226
mini chocolate meringues 166
mini chocolate sandwich cakes 42
mocha cream muffins 24
pistachio & chocolate meringues 172
pistachio & white chocolate florentines 70
pistachio & white chocolate meringues 162
real chocolate brownies 124
rich chocolate macaroons 176
rich chocolate mocha brownies 124
sticky chocolate orange cakes 220
triple chocolate pretzels 78
very chocolatey muffins 20
white chocolate & lavender cups 44
white chocolate & macadamia cupcakes 36

white chocolate & mint discs 166
white chocolate coconut muffins 60
white chocolate crunchies 44
white chocolate drops 82
white chocolate fancies 192
white chocolate frosting 210
white chocolate raspberry cupcakes 26
white chocolate sauce 142
white chocolate scones with ginger butter 188
white chocolate strawberry muffins 60
wiggly worm 222
chocolate beans:
sweetie-topped cookie cakes 214
Christmas cake stack 224
Christmas cakes, mini 64
Christmas tree cakes 6
churros 142
cider-glazed apple slice 106
cinnamon:
cinnamon fruit puffs 150
honey, grape & cinnamon tartlets 140
cocoa powder:
fiery chocolate cupcakes 54
mini chocolate sandwich cakes 42
coconut:
coconut & ginger flapjacks 200
lamingtons 206
sweetie-topped cookie cakes 214
white chocolate coconut muffins 60
coconut, creamed:
coconut-frosted pineapple slice 108

coconut milk: coconut & rosewater slice 108
coffee:
almond-coffee cake 116
chocolate tiramisu cups 58
espresso madeleines with coffee glaze 204
marsala raisin coffee muffins 24
mini cappuccino cakes 42
mocha cream palmiers 156
rich chocolate mocha brownies 124
coffee liqueur: chocolate eclairs & cream liqueur 134
cookies:
baby shower cookies 94
cookies & cream fudge 120
happy faces 228
pumpkin-face cookies 88
puppies & kittens 216
scrabble cookies 96
trick or treat ghosties 232
walnut oat cookies 84
wise old owls 232
cornflakes: milk chocolate crackles 226
courgette & lime cupcakes 50
cranberries:
cranberry & orange scones 186
cranberry mincemeat cupcakes 46
florentines 70
sweetie-topped cookie cakes 214
cream:
almond praline buns 130
crème pâtissière buns 130
cupcakes: birthday cake

stack 224
chocolate fudge cupcakes 30
chocolate tiramisu cups 58
Christmas cake stack 224
courgette & lime cupcakes 50
cranberry mincemeat cupcakes 46
honey & pine nut cakes 56
lemon & limincello cupcakes 18
lemon meringue cupcakes 164
maple butter pecan cupcakes 36
marshmallow cream cakes 26
mini mint fudge cakes 32
mini minted cupcakes 32
mini trifle cups 58
peanut caramel cupcakes 56
redcurrant meringue cupcakes 164
rhubarb & orange cupcakes 18
white chocolate & macadamia cupcakes 36
white chocolate raspberry cupcakes 26
wiggly worm 222

dates: date & fresh ginger sticks 152
sticky toffee & date slice 106
dip, glossy chocolate 78

eclairs: chocolate eclairs & cream liqueur 134
eggs: crème pâtissière 130
espresso madeleines with coffee glaze 204

festive tree biscuits 90
figs: honeyed fig cakes 196
filo pastries:
  blueberry & cream cheese tartlets 140
  chocolate filo twiglets 152
  honey, grape & cinnamon tartlets 140
  mini nectarine & blueberry tarts 154
  plum tripiti 136
flapjacks:
  banana flapjack bites 200
  coconut & ginger flapjacks 200
florentines 70
French macaroons 174
friands:
  blueberry friands 22
  hazelnut & apricot friands 22
frosting:
  lime frosting 104
  tangy yogurt frosting 214
  white chocolate frosting 210
fruit, dried:
  cranberry mincemeat cupcakes 46
  mini Christmas cakes 64
  mini simnel cakes 62
fudge:
  chocolate fudge cupcakes 30
  chocolate, orange & walnut fudge 120
  cookies & cream fudge 120
  mini mint fudge cakes 32
  vanilla fudge nuggets 80
fun letter biscuits 218

ginger: apricot & ginger cakes 34
birthday bundles 86
chocolate ginger

cheesecakes 28
coconut & ginger flapjacks 200
date & fresh ginger sticks 152
ginger & nougat sables 76
ginger cream biscuits 86
ginger muffin slice 104
ginger profiteroles 148
mango & ginger cakes 112
mascarpone & ginger frosting 180
parsnip, ginger & hazelnut cakes 194
pomegranate & ginger slice 118
tropical ginger cake 104
white chocolate scones with vanilla & ginger butter 188
gingerbread:
  sultana & lemon gingerbread 118
  window cookies 234
gluten-free:
  almond macaroons 178
  banoffi bites 52
  chocolate brownies 100
  gooseberry & elderflower muffins 38
grapes: honey, grape & cinnamon tartlets 140

happy faces 228
hazelnuts:
  chocolate filo twiglets 152
  hazelnut & apricot friands 22
  hazelnut & orange fingers 72
  parsnip, ginger & hazelnut cakes 194
honey:
  honey & pine nut cakes 56
  honey, grape &

cinnamon tartlets 140
honeyed fig cakes 196
honeycomb bars: white chocolate crunchies 44

ice cream, mascarpone & vanilla 154
icing:
  homemade ready-to-roll icing 96
  royal icing 234

jam: homemade strawberry jam 110

lamingtons 206
lavender:
  lavender tea scones 186
  white chocolate & lavender cups 44
lemons:
  citrus baklava 144
  lemon & cardamom shortbreads 74
  lemon & limincello cupcakes 18
  lemon drizzle bites 116
  lemon glazed cardamom madeleines 204
  lemon meringue cupcakes 164
  tangy lemon squares 138
limes:
  courgette & lime cupcakes 50
  lime frosting 104
  meringue-frosted lime squares 138
  papaya, lime & mango tartlets 158
limoncello liqueur: lemon & limincello cupcakes 18
little dinos 230

macadamia nuts: white chocolate & macadamia cupcakes 36
macaroons:
  almond & white

chocolate kisses 178
French macaroons 174
gluten-free almond macaroons 178
rich chocolate macaroons 176
madeleines:
  espresso madeleines with coffee glaze 204
  lemon glazed cardamom madeleines 204
magic wands 218
mango:
  mango & ginger cakes 112
  papaya, lime & mango tartlets 158
maple syrup:
  maple & walnut tartlets 128
  maple butter pecan cupcakes 36
marmalade: sticky chocolate orange cakes 220
marsala raisin coffee muffins 24
marshmallows:
  chocolate fridge cakes 226
  marshmallow cream cakes 26
  mini marshmallow flowers 94
marzipan:
  Christmas tree cakes 64
  mini Christmas cakes 64
  stollen slice 114
meringue:
  banoffee meringues 170
  brown sugar meringues 162
  lemon meringue cupcakes 164
  meringue-frosted lime squares 138
  mini chocolate meringues 166
  pistachio & chocolate